SELECTED NUMERICAL METHODS AND COMPUTER PROGRAMS

FOR CHEMICAL ENGINEERS

Huan-Yang Chang
And
Ira Earl Over

STERLING
SWIFT publishing company
p.o. box 188
manchaca, texas 78652

To

Our families

ISBN 0-88408-131-1

Preface

This book is application oriented and is intended for
those who already know the elements of FORTRAN programming or
who are learning computer programming concurrently. Some of
the well-known numerical methods are described briefly with
minimal derivations. Special emphasis is focused on the
application of the numerical methods to the solution of typical
chemical engineering problems. Each method is illustrated with
worked out sample programs to demonstrate the areas of application and to show how problems should be formulated for
solution on a computer. Unless the methods are straightforward,
FORTRAN programs are supplemented with flow charts describing
sequences of development and programming. It is the authors'
hope that enough is covered to permit the beginning chemical
engineering student to write simple programs of his own with
some degree of confidence.

There are certain difficulties and pitfalls associated
with numerical computations. They are pointed out wherever
appropriate. The user should be aware of them. Often there
are a number of methods available for solving a particular
problem, with one method giving better results than another.
The examples in this book will reduce confusion and will
provide beginners with insight into some of the most commonly
used techniques to computer programming. It is impossible to

cover all aspects. The authors do not attempt to exhaust the areas of application.

In the learning process all of us go through the periods of groping, appreciating, and finally, comprehending. Hopefully, the insight you obtain from this introductory text will stimulate interest in more sophisticated methods and will encourage you to continue your own development beyond the limitations of this book.

Since time-sharing systems have become progressively more popular, all programs were written in FORTRAN Extended Version IV for use on a time-sharing terminal. The format-free approach was adopted for handling inputs because it is the more convenient, however, all outputs were provided with formats as desired. All listed programs have been tested and run on the University of Lowell CDC Cyber 71 computer system. The authors are indebted to the Computer Center of the University of Lowell for the use of its facilities.

H. Y. C.

I. E. O.

TABLE OF CONTENTS

iv

LIST OF TABLES

Chapter 1

Solution of a Nonlinear Equation

1.1 Method of Bisection

We consider the case in which the function has one and only one root in the interval (a, b).

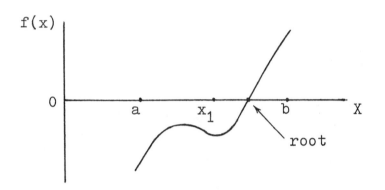

Figure 1-1. A plot of f(x) vs. x

The bisection or interval halving method is a simple systematic way of finding a root. The following procedure may be used to locate the root.

(a) Evaluate $f(x_1)$ at the midpoint of the interval, $x_1=(a+b)/2$.

(b) If $f(x_1)$ is zero, x_1 is the root. However, this outcome is not likely.

(c) if $f(x_1)>0$, the root must lie in the interval (a, x_1).

   Reset b = x_1.

   If $f(x_1)<0$, the root must lie in the interval (x_1, b).

   Reset a = x_1.

   In either case the interval is cut in half.

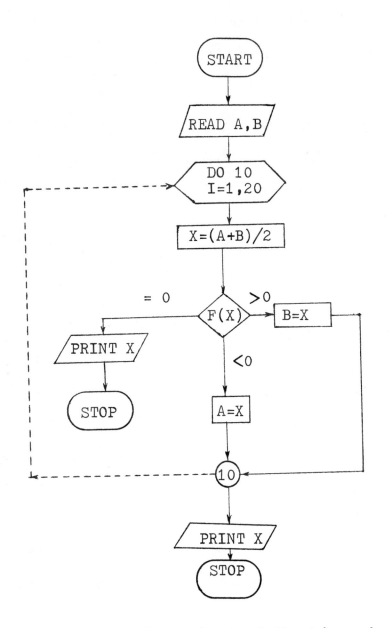

Figure 1-2. Flow chart of the bisection method

2

(d) Select that half which contains the root and repeat steps
(a) through (c) for further bisection. After twenty
iterations the size of the interval is very small, and
the midpoint of the final interval will be accepted as a
satisfactory approximation of the root.

The flow chart for the method of bisection is found in
Figure 1-2. The flow chart shows how the successive intervals
are reset, with the root always lying in the subinterval to be
bisected next.

EXAMPLE 1.1-1. The Underwood Equation

In a distillation calculation we often use the Underwood
equation (1948) to calculate the minimum reflux ratio, and in
doing so we need to solve the following expression:

$$F(\phi) = \frac{2.3(.10)}{2.3 - \phi} + \frac{1.75(.13)}{1.75 - \phi} + \frac{1.45(.25)}{1.45 - \phi} + \frac{1.0(.23)}{1.0 - \phi}$$

$$+ \frac{0.9(.15)}{0.9 - \phi} + \frac{0.83(.08)}{0.83 - \phi} + \frac{0.65(.06)}{0.65 - \phi} = 0.$$

There are a number of roots to the above equation. We wish to
find a root such that $1.0 < \phi < 1.45$. Solve the problem by the
method of bisection.

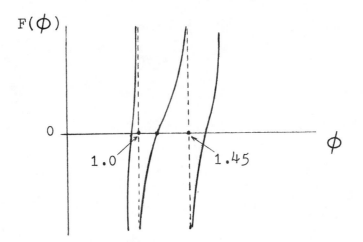

Figure 1-3.   Root of $F(\phi)$ between 1.0 and 1.45

Refer to Figure 1-3.   Note that the ordinates at $\phi = 1.0$ and 1.45 are asymptotes, and that $F(\phi) \rightarrow -\infty$ as $\phi \rightarrow 1.0$ and $F(\phi) \rightarrow \infty$ as $\phi \rightarrow 1.45$ in the open interval $1.0 < \phi < 1.45$.

PROGRAM BISECT

Description of Input/Output

The given function is first defined.

PHILL -(input) the lower limit of phi

PHIUL -(input) the upper limit of phi

PHI -(output) the root of the function in the given interval

A format-free approach is used for all inputs.   PROGRAM BISECT (see Table 1-1) was executed to solve Example 1.1-1. Table 1-2 lists computer printout for twenty iterations, at the end of which PHI = 1.185001.   The results of intermediate

4

Table 1-1. PROGRAM BISECT

```
00100       PROGRAM BISECT(INPUT,OUTPUT)
00110C
00120C      DEFINE FUNCTION
00130C
00140       F(PHI)=0.23/(2.3-PHI)+0.2275/(1.75-PHI)+0.3625/(1.45-PHI)
00150+      +0.23/(1.-PHI)+0.135/(0.9-PHI)+0.0664/(0.83-PHI)
00160+      +0.039/(0.65-PHI)
00170C
00180C      THE BISECTION METHOD
00190C
00200       READ*,PHILL,PHIUL
00210       PRINT 5
00220     5 FORMAT(//10X,"PHILL",5X,"PHIUL",5X,"PHI")
00230       DO 10 I=1,20
00240       PHI=0.5*(PHILL+PHIUL)
00250       PRINT 25,PHILL,PHIUL,PHI
00260    25 FORMAT(5X,3F10.6)
00270       FPHI=F(PHI)
00280       IF(FPHI) 20,40,30
00290    20 PHILL=PHI
00300       GO TO 10
00310    30 PHIUL=PHI
00320    10 CONTINUE
00330    40 PRINT 50,PHI
00340    50 FORMAT(//5X,"AFTER 20 ITERATIONS PHI =",F10.6)
00350       STOP
00360       END
```

Table 1-2. An application of PROGRAM BISECT

DATA INPUT AT TIME OF EXECUTION
? 1.0, 1.45
OUTPUT

PHILL	PHIUL	PHI
1.000000	1.450000	1.225000
1.000000	1.225000	1.112500
1.112500	1.225000	1.168750
1.168750	1.225000	1.196875
1.168750	1.196875	1.182813
1.182813	1.196875	1.189844
1.182813	1.189844	1.186328
1.182813	1.186328	1.184570
1.184570	1.186328	1.185449
1.184570	1.185449	1.185010
1.184570	1.185010	1.184790
1.184790	1.185010	1.184900
1.184900	1.185010	1.184955
1.184955	1.185010	1.184982
1.184982	1.185010	1.184996
1.184996	1.185010	1.185003
1.184996	1.185003	1.184999
1.184999	1.185003	1.185001
1.184999	1.185001	1.185000
1.185000	1.185001	1.185001

AFTER 20 ITERATIONS PHI = 1.185001

calculations have been included to show the reset of the intervals.

1.2 Method of Successive Substitutions

Solution of a single equation by the method of successive substitutions involves the following steps:

(a) Arrange the equation in the form $x = f(x)$.

(b) Start with an initial guess of $x = x_1$. A second, and hopefully improved, value of $x = x_2$ is obtained by solving for $x_2 = f(x_1)$. In general, the following successive substitutions are made: $x_{n+1} = f(x_n)$.

(c) Convergence is obtained if the condition $\left| x_{n+1} - x_n \right| < \epsilon$ *
is satisfied, where ϵ is a specified tolerance limit. The choice of ϵ depends on the circumstances.

(d) Successive substitutions when applied to some functions will not lead to a solution. Therefore, the search in a code should be terminated if no root has been found after a specified maximum number of iterations.

EXAMPLE 1.2-1. <u>The Virial Equation of State</u>

The virial equation of state truncated to three terms provides an excellent representation of P-V-T relationship for a gas at moderate pressures. It is given by

---

*See Appendix at the end of chapter 1 for explanations.

$$\frac{PV}{RT} = 1 + \frac{B}{V} + \frac{C}{V^2},$$

(1.2-1)

where P = pressure,

   V = specific volume,

   R = gas constant,

   T = absolute temperature,

   B, C = virial coefficients.

Estimate the specific volume of sulfur dioxide at 75 atm and 157.5°C. The virial coefficients are

   $B = -159 \text{ cm}^3/\text{g-mole}$,

   $C = 9000 \text{ (cm)}^6/(\text{g-mole})^2$.

Solve by the method of successive substitutions.

   FORTRAN programming requires that the virial equation be rearranged to the form

   V = R*T/P*(1 + B/V + C/V**2).

An initial guess of V is obtained by using the ideal gas equation V = R*T/P.

PROGRAM VIRIAL1

Description of Input/Output

B   -(input) the second virial coefficient $(\text{cm}^3/\text{g-mole})$

C   -(input) the third virial coefficient $(\text{cm}^3/\text{g-mole})^2$

R   -(input) the gas constant = 82.05 $(\text{cm}^3)(\text{atm})/((\text{g-mole})(^\circ\text{K}))$

Table 1-3. PROGRAM VIRIAL1

```
00100        PROGRAM VIRIAL1(INPUT,OUTPUT)
00110C
00120C       THIS PROGRAM SOLVES THE VIRIAL EQUATION OF STATE
00130C       BY THE METHOD OF SUCCESSIVE SUBSTITUTIONS.
00140C
00150C
00160C       DEFINE FUNCTION
00170C
00180        F(V)=R*T/P*(1.+B/V+C/V**2)
00190C
00200C       DATA INPUT
00210C
00220        READ*,B,C,R,T,P,IMAX,EPS
00230        PRINT 1,B,C,R,T,P,EPS
00240      1 FORMAT(//5X,"B =",F10.2," CU CM/G-MOLE"/
00250+       5X,"C =",F10.2," (CU CM/G-MOLE)**2"/
00260+       5X,"R =",F10.2," (CU CM)(ATM)/((G-MOLE)(DEG K))"/
00270+       5X,"T =",F10.2," DEG C"/5X,"P =",F10.2," ATM"/
00280+       5X,"EPS =",F10.6)
00290        T=T+273.15
00300C
00310C       INITIAL GUESS OF V BY THE IDEAL GAS EQUATION
00320C
00330        V=R*T/P
00340        PRINT 2
00350      2 FORMAT(//14X,"V",11X,"VNEW")
00360C
00370C       METHOD OF SUCCESSIVE SUBSTITUTIONS
00380C
00390        DO 10 I=1,IMAX
00400        VNEW=F(V)
00410C
00420C       CHECK CONVERGENCE
00430C
00440        IF(ABS(VNEW-V).LT.EPS) GO TO 5
00450        PRINT 4,V,VNEW
00460      4 FORMAT(2E15.5)
00470     10 V=VNEW
00480        PRINT 20,IMAX
00490     20 FORMAT(//5X,"CONVERGENCE FAILED AFTER",I5," ITERATIONS.")
00500        GO TO 100
00510C
00520C       CONVERGENCE ACHIEVED.  PRINT ANSWER .
00530C
00540      5 PRINT 6,VNEW
00550      6 FORMAT(//5X,"VOLUME =",E15.5," CU CM/G-MOLE")
00560    100 STOP
00570        END
```

Table 1-4. An application of PROGRAM VIRIAL1

DATA INPUT AT TIME OF EXECUTION

? -159., 9000., 82.05, 157.5, 75., 50, .01

OUTPUT

```
     B  =     -159.00 CU CM/G-MOLE
     C  =     9000.00 (CU CM/G-MOLE)**2
     R  =       82.05 (CU CM)(ATM)/((G-MOLE)(DEG K))
     T  =      157.50 DEG C
     P  =       75.00 ATM
     EPS =        .010000
```

V	VNEW
.47113E+03	.33123E+03
.33123E+03	.28362E+03
.28362E+03	.25973E+03
.25973E+03	.24557E+03
.24557E+03	.23640E+03
.23640E+03	.23013E+03
.23013E+03	.22568E+03
.22568E+03	.22246E+03
.22246E+03	.22007E+03
.22007E+03	.21829E+03
.21829E+03	.21695E+03
.21695E+03	.21593E+03
.21593E+03	.21516E+03
.21516E+03	.21456E+03
.21456E+03	.21411E+03
.21411E+03	.21376E+03
.21376E+03	.21349E+03
.21349E+03	.21328E+03
.21328E+03	.21312E+03
.21312E+03	.21299E+03
.21299E+03	.21289E+03
.21289E+03	.21282E+03
.21282E+03	.21276E+03
.21276E+03	.21272E+03
.21272E+03	.21268E+03
.21268E+03	.21266E+03
.21266E+03	.21264E+03
.21264E+03	.21262E+03
.21262E+03	.21261E+03

```
     VOLUME =      .21260E+03 CU CM/G-MOLE
```

T   -(input) the temperature ($^{\circ}$C).(The computer program
         converts the temperature to $^{\circ}$K.)

P   -(input) the pressure (atm)

IMAX   -(input) the maximun number of iterations to be performed
         before a root is found

EPS   -(input) the tolerance limit

V   -(intermediate calculation) the estimated volume
         (cm^3/g-mole)

VNEW   -(output) the accepted value of the specific volume
         (cm^3/g-mole)

    By manual calculation using the ideal gas equation, we
found that V was of the order of several hundred cubic centi-
meters per g-mole. A tolerance limit ϵ = 0.01 should be
satisfactory. PROGRAM VIRIAL1 (see Table 1-3) was run on
the time-sharing terminal of the CDC Cyber 71 computer system.
Convergence was obtained after twenty-nine iterations and the
solution was

$$V = 212.60 \text{ } cm^3/\text{g-mole}.$$

The computer printout was given in Table 1-4.

1.3 Newton's Method

    We wish to find the root of $f(x) = 0$. Assume that x_1 is
the initial guess of the root. As shown in Figure 1-4, we
draw a line tangent to the curve at $x = x_1$, intersecting the
abscissa at x_2. We have

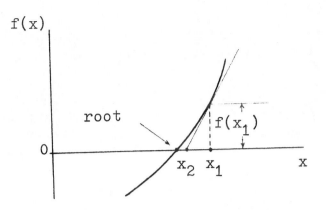

Figure 1-4. Root determination by Newton's method

$$f'(x_1) = \frac{f(x_1)}{x_1 - x_2} . \qquad (1.3\text{-}1)$$

Rearranging,

$$x_2 = x_1 - \frac{f(x_1)}{f'(x_1)} . \qquad (1.3\text{-}2)$$

Newton's method generally converges rapidly to the desired solution. However, there is no guarantee that convergence is always obtained. Therefore, provisions should be made to terminate the iteration at the first sign of divergence. An outline of the iterative procedure is given as follows:

(a) Make an initial guess $x = x_1$ of the root.

(b) Evaluate $f(x_1)$ and $f'(x_1)$; the new estimate of the root is given by

$$x_2 = x_1 - \frac{f(x_1)}{f'(x_1)} .$$

In general,

$$x_{n+1} = x_n - \frac{f(x_n)}{f'(x_n)} .$$

(c) Convergence is achieved if $\left| x_{n+1} - x_n \right| < \epsilon$.

   If not, repeat steps (b) and (c).

(d) Alternately, the search is terminated if the root has not
   been found after a specified number of iterations.

EXAMPLE 1.3-1. The Virial Equation of State

   Rework Example 1.2-1, using Newton's method.

PROGRAM VIRIAL2

Description of Input/Output

They are the same as listed under PROGRAM VIRIAL1.

   PROGRAM VIRIAL2 (see Table 1-5) uses Newton's method to
solve the virial equation of state. With $\epsilon = 0.01$ the program
completes five iterations to converge to the solution, as
compared with twenty-nine iterations for the method of successive substitutions. Although Newton's method generally
converges rapidly, the calculation per iteration is longer,
since it is necessary to evaluate both the function and its
derivative. The solution is

$$V = 212.56 \text{ cm}^3/\text{g-mole},$$

which agrees with that obtained from PROGRAM VIRIAL1. The
computer printout is given in Table 1-6.

Table 1-5. PROGRAM VIRIAL2

```
00100        PROGRAM VIRIAL2(INPUT,OUTPUT)
00110C
00120C       THIS PROGRAM SOLVES THE VIRIAL EQUATION OF STATE
00130C       BY THE NEWTON'S METHOD.
00140C
00150C
00160C       DEFINE FUNCTION
00170C
00180        F(V)=1.+B/V+C/V**2-P*V/(R*T)
00190        DF(V)=-B/V**2-2.*C/V**3-P/(R*T)
00200C
00210C       DATA INPUT
00220C
00230        READ*,B,C,R,T,P,IMAX,EPS
00240        PRINT 1,B,C,R,T,P,EPS
00250      1 FORMAT(//5X,"B =",F10.2," CU CM/G-MOLE"/
00260+       5X,"C =",F10.2," (CU CM/G-MOLE)**2"/
00270+       5X,"R =",F10.2," (CU CM)(ATM)/((G-MOLE)(DEG K))"/
00280+       5X,"T =",F10.2," DEG C"/5X,"P =",F10.2," ATM"/
00290+       5X,"EPS =",F10.6)
00300        T=T+273.15
00310C
00320C       INITIAL GUESS OF V BY THE IDEAL GAS EQUATION
00330C
00340        V=R*T/P
00350        PRINT 2
00360      2 FORMAT(//14X,"V",11X,"VNEW")
00370C
00380C       NEWTON'S METHOD
00390C
00400        DO 10 I=1,IMAX
00410        FV=F(V)
00420        DFV=DF(V)
00430        VNEW=V-FV/DFV
00440C
00450C       CHECK CONVERGENCE
00460C
00470        IF(ABS(VNEW-V).LT.EPS) GO TO 5
00480        PRINT 4,V,VNEW
00490      4 FORMAT(2E15.5)
00500     10 V=VNEW
00510        PRINT 20,IMAX
00520     20 FORMAT(//5X,"CONVERGENCE FAILED AFTER",I5," ITERATIONS.")
00530        GO TO 100
00540C
00550C       CONVERGENCE ACHIEVED.  PRINT ANSWER .
00560C
00570      5 PRINT 6,VNEW
00580      6 FORMAT(//5X,"VOLUME =",E15.5," CU CM/G-MOLE")
00590    100 STOP
00600        END
```

14

Table 1-6. An application of PROGRAM VIRIAL2

DATA INPUT AT TIME OF EXECUTION

? -159., 9000., 82.05, 157.5, 75., 50, .01
OUTPUT

```
     B =    -159.00 CU CM/G-MOLE
     C =    9000.00 (CU CM/G-MOLE)**2
     R =      82.05 (CU CM)(ATM)/((G-MOLE)(DEG K))
     T =     157.50 DEG C
     P =      75.00 ATM
     EPS =     .010000


              V               VNEW
     .47113E+03        .28300E+03
     .28300E+03        .22916E+03
     .22916E+03        .21416E+03
     .21416E+03        .21258E+03
     .21258E+03        .21256E+03


     VOLUME =       .21256E+03 CU CM/G-MOLE
```

EXAMPLE 1.3-2. <u>Bubble-Point Temperature</u>

A liquid containing n components is in equilibrium with the vapor at total pressure P. The vapor-liquid equilibrium ratio constant is defined as

$$K_i = y_i/x_i, \qquad (1.3-3)$$

where x_i = mole fraction of component i in the liquid,

y_i = mole fraction of component i in the vapor.

Assume that K is a function of temperature and pressure and that at the given pressure K-values can be represented by

$$\ln K_i = A_i + B_i T + C_i T^2, \qquad (1.3-4)$$

where A_i, B_i, and C_i are constants; T is temperature (°F). The problem is, given P and x_i's, compute the equilibrium temperature, which is the bubble point. The given pressure is at 1 atm. Other numerical data are

x_i	A_i	B_i	C_i
.1104	-2.99279	2.2270×10^{-2}	-1.8669×10^{-5}
.2829	-5.90449	2.9968×10^{-2}	-2.7439×10^{-5}
.6067	-8.72046	3.7367×10^{-2}	-3.5124×10^{-5}

From the definition of the K-values we have

$$y_i = K_i x_i. \qquad (1.3-5)$$

Since the sum of mole fractions in the vapor should equal unity, we obtain

$$\sum y_i = \sum K_i x_i = \sum \left[\text{Exp}(A_i + B_i T + C_i T^2) \right] x_i = 1. \qquad (1.3\text{-}6)$$

Upon rearrangement the above equation yields

$$F(T) = \sum K_i x_i - 1 = 0. \qquad (1.3\text{-}7)$$

Now the problem of finding the bubble-point temperature has been reduced to that of finding the root of $F(T) = 0$. We use Newton's method. Compute the first derivative of the function

$$
\begin{aligned}
F'(T) &= \frac{d}{dT}\left[F(T) \right] = \frac{d}{dT}\left(\sum K_i x_i - 1 \right) \\
&= \sum \text{Exp}(A_i + B_i T + C_i T^2)\left[x_i(B_i + 2C_i T) \right] \\
&= \sum K_i x_i (B_i + 2C_i T). \qquad (1.3\text{-}8)
\end{aligned}
$$

The computation proceeds as follows:

(a) Assume T.(The initial value is read in as an input.)

(b) Compute K_i's, $F(T)$, and $F'(T)$.

(c) Update the temperature estimation by Newton's method,

$$T_{new} = T_{old} - \frac{F(T_{old})}{F'(T_{old})}.$$

(d) Check for convergence. If $\left| T_{new} - T_{old} \right| < \epsilon$, the root is found. If not, set $T_{old} = T_{new}$ and repeat steps (b) through (d) to find another T_{new}.

PROGRAM BBLT

Description of Input/Output

N   -(input) the number of components

X   -(input) one-dimensional array containing the liquid
         mole fractions

A,B,C -(input) one-dimensional arrays containing the coeffi-
        cients of the K-value equation

T   -(input) the initial estimate of the temperature

TNEW   -(output) the bubble-point temperature

Y   -(output) one-dimensional array containing the vapor
         mole fractions in equilibrium with the liquid

K   -(output) one-dimensional array containing the K-values
         at the bubble point temperature

PROGRAM BBLT (see Table 1-7) was run on the time-sharing
terminal of the CDC Cyber 71 computer system to solve Example
1.3-2. The initial guess of the temperature was T = 250°F, and
the tolerance limit ϵ was set at $\pm 0.01^{\circ}$F for any two successive
calculations. Since we usually would not require the tempera-
ture to be accurate within $\pm 0.01^{\circ}$F, $\epsilon = 0.01$ should be satisfactory for this calculation. The program completed three
iterations to converge to the solution. The answer was

The bubble-point temperature = 262.99°F.

The computer printout in Table 1-8 also gave the final value
of F(T) = 0.00009366. Since it was close enough to zero, the
value of the bubble-point temperature was accepted. The sum
of y_i's did not equal 1.0. The small deviation was caused
by rounding off the decimals.

Table 1-7. PROGRAM BBLT

```
00100      PROGRAM BBLT(INPUT,OUTPUT)
00110      REAL K(10)
00120      DIMENSION A(10),B(10),C(10),X(10),Y(10)
00130C
00140C     DATA INPUT
00150C
00160      READ*,N
00170      READ*,(X(I),I=1,N)
00180      READ*,(A(I),B(I),C(I),I=1,N)
00190      READ*,T
00200C
00210C     CALCULATING THE BUBBLE POINT BY NEWTON'S METHOD
00220C
00230      PRINT 10
00240   10 FORMAT(//" THE VALUES OF TOLD, FT, AND TNEW ARE"/)
00250C
00260C     STARTING NEWTON'S METHOD ITERATIONS
00270C
00280    1 FT=-1.
00290      DFT=0.
00300      DO 2 I=1,N
00310      K(I)=EXP(A(I)+B(I)*T+C(I)*T*T)
00320      FT=FT+X(I)*K(I)
00330    2 DFT=DFT+X(I)*K(I)*(B(I)+2.*C(I)*T)
00340      TOLD=T
00350      TNEW=T-FT/DFT
00360C
00370C     CHECK CONVERGENCE
00380C
00390      IF(ABS(TNEW-T).LT..01) GO TO 4
00400      PRINT 3,TOLD,FT,TNEW
00410    3 FORMAT(F10.2,E16.8,F10.2)
00420C
00430C     UPDATE T AND MAKE ANOTHER TRY
00440C
00450      T=TNEW
00460      GO TO 1
00470    4 PRINT 3,TOLD,FT,TNEW
00480      DO 5 I=1,N
00490    5 Y(I)=K(I)*X(I)
00500      PRINT 6,TNEW
00510    6 FORMAT(//5X,"BUBBLE POINT TEMPERATURE =",F10.2)
00520      PRINT 7,(X(I),Y(I),K(I),I=1,N)
00530    7 FORMAT(//5X,"X(I)",6X,"Y(I)",6X,"K(I)"//(3F10.4))
00540      STOP
00550      END
```

Table 1-8. An application of PROGRAM BBLT

DATA INPUT AT TIME OF EXECUTION

? 3
? .1104, .2829, .6067
? -2.99279, 2.2270E-2, -1.8669E-5
? -5.90449, 2.9968E-2, -2.7439E-5
? -8.72046, 3.7367E-2, -3.5124E-5
? 250.

OUTPUT

THE VALUES OF TOLD, FT, AND TNEW ARE

250.00	-.17398103E+00	264.06
264.06	.15485563E-01	263.00
263.00	.93664937E-04	262.99

BUBBLE POINT TEMPERATURE =   262.99

X(I)	Y(I)	K(I)
.1104	.5322	4.8207
.2829	.3062	1.0824
.6067	.1617	.2665

EXAMPLE 1.3-3. Dew-Point Temperature

In Example 1.3-2, if the total pressure P and the vapor composition y_i's are given, then the equilibrium temperature is called the dew-point temperature. Rework Example 1.3-2. The y_i values are 0.5321, 0.3062, and 0.1617.(Notice that we have made a slight adjustment to make the sum of y_i's equal unity.)   The pressure is 1 atm.   The coefficients A_i, B_i, and C_i of the K-value equation are given in Example 1.3-2.   Find the dew-point temperature and the corresponding x_i's.

In this case we start by computing the x_i's,

$$x_i = \frac{y_i}{K_i} .$$ (1.3-9)

Since the sum of mole fractions in the liquid should equal unity, we have

$$\sum x_i = \sum \frac{y_i}{K_i} = \sum \frac{y_i}{Exp(A_i + B_i T + C_i T^2)} = 1.$$ (1.3-10)

Rearranging,

$$F(T) = \sum \frac{y_i}{K_i} - 1 = 0.$$ (1.3-11)

We use Newton's method to find the root of $F(T) = 0$.   The first derivative of the function is

$$F'(T) = \frac{d}{dT}\Big[F(T)\Big] = -\sum \frac{y_i(B_i + 2C_iT)}{K_i} \ . \qquad (1.3\text{-}12)$$

The computation procedure is similar to that of finding the bubble-point temperature.

PROGRAM DEWT

Description of Input/Output

N   -(input) the number of components

Y   -(input) one-dimensional array containing the vapor
          mole fractions

A,B,C -(input) one-dimensional arrays containing the coeffi-
          cients of the K-value equation

T   -(input) the initial estimate of the temperature

TNEW   -(output) the dew-point temperature

X   -(output) one-dimensional array containing the liquid
          mole fractions in equilibrium with the vapor

K   -(output) one-dimensional array containing the K-values
          at the dew-point temperature

PROGRAM DEWT (see Table 1-9) was run to solve Example 1.3-3. The initial estimate of the temperature was T = 250°F, and the tolerance limit ϵ was ±0.01. After four iterations the solution was

The dew-point temperature = 263.00°F.

Table 1-10 lists the computer printout.

Table 1-9. PROGRAM DEWT

```
00100        PROGRAM DEWT(INPUT,OUTPUT)
00110        REAL K(10)
00120        DIMENSION A(10),B(10),C(10),X(10),Y(10)
00130C
00140C       DATA INPUT
00150C
00160        READ*,N
00170        READ*,(Y(I),I=1,N)
00180        READ*,(A(I),B(I),C(I),I=1,N)
00190        READ*,T
00200C
00210C       CALCULATING THE DEW POINT BY NEWTON'S METHOD
00220C
00230        PRINT 10
00240     10 FORMAT(//" THE VALUES OF TOLD, FT, AND TNEW ARE"/)
00250C
00260C       STARTING NEWTON'S METHOD ITERATIONS
00270C
00280      1 FT=-1.
00290        DFT=0.
00300        DO 2 I=1,N
00310        K(I)=EXP(A(I)+B(I)*T+C(I)*T*T)
00320        FT=FT+Y(I)/K(I)
00330      2 DFT=DFT-Y(I)*(B(I)+2.*C(I)*T)/K(I)
00340        TOLD=T
00350        TNEW=T-FT/DFT
00360C
00370C       CHECK CONVERGENCE
00380C
00390        IF(ABS(TNEW-T).LT..01) GO TO 4
00400        PRINT 3,TOLD,FT,TNEW
00410      3 FORMAT(F10.2,E16.8,F10.2)
00420C
00430C       UPDATE T AND MAKE ANOTHER TRY
00440C
00450        T=TNEW
00460        GO TO 1
00470      4 PRINT 3,TOLD,FT,TNEW
00480        DO 5 I=1,N
00490      5 X(I)=Y(I)/K(I)
00500        PRINT 6,TNEW
00510      6 FORMAT(//5X,"DEW POINT TEMPERATURE =",F10.2)
00520        PRINT 7,(Y(I),X(I),K(I),I=1,N)
00530      7 FORMAT(//5X,"Y(I)",6X,"X(I)",6X,"K(I)"//(3F10.4))
00540        STOP
00550        END
```

Table 1-10. An application of PROGRAM DEWT

DATA INPUT AT TIME OF EXECUTION

? 3
? .5321, .3062, .1617
? -2.99279, 2.2270E-2, -1.8669E-5
? -5.90449, 2.9968E-2, -2.7439E-5
? -8.72046, 3.7367E-2, -3.5124E-5
? 250.
OUTPUT

THE VALUES OF TOLD, FT, AND TNEW ARE

TOLD	FT	TNEW
250.00	.25831438E+00	261.33
261.33	.29266542E-01	262.97
262.97	.50272817E-03	263.00
263.00	.15488255E-06	263.00

DEW POINT TEMPERATURE =   263.00

Y(I)	X(I)	K(I)
.5321	.1104	4.8208
.3062	.2829	1.0824
.1617	.6067	.2665

EXAMPLE 1.3-4. <u>Flash Vaporization</u>

Consider the process represented in Figure 1-5. It involves the flash vaporization of a feed of given composition at a specified temperature and pressure into a vapor and a liquid in equilibrium. The problem is to determine the fractions of vapor and liquid formed and the compositions of the respective streams. The feed composition and the K-values are

z_i	K_i
.40	4.6431
.30	1.0328
.30	0.2517

The pressure is at 1 atm and the temperature is 260°F.

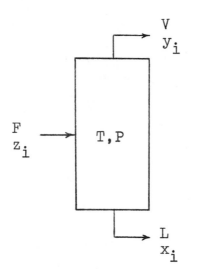

Figure 1-5. Flash Vaporization

Let F = flow rate of the feed stream,

   V = flow rate of the vapor product,

   L = flow rate of the liquid product,

   x_i, y_i, z_i = mole fractions of component i in the liquid, vapor, and feed streams, respectively,

   K_i = vapor-liquid equilibrium ratio = y_i/x_i.

The material balance equations are

$$F = V + L, \qquad\qquad (1.3-13)$$

$$Fz_i = Vy_i + Lx_i. \qquad\qquad (1.3-14)$$

Since the vapor and liquid streams are in equilibrium

$$y_i = K_i x_i. \qquad\qquad (1.3-15)$$

Eliminating L and y, and solving for x,

$$x_i = \frac{z_i}{1 + \frac{V}{F}(K_i - 1)}. \qquad\qquad (1.3-16)$$

Similarly,

$$y_i = \frac{K_i z_i}{1 + \frac{V}{F}(K_i - 1)}. \qquad\qquad (1.3-17)$$

If we choose 1 mole of feed as our basis, then F = 1 and V/F = V. Eqs. (1.3-16) and (1.3-17) can be written as

$$x_i = \frac{z_i}{1 + V(K_i - 1)} , \tag{1.3-18}$$

$$y_i = \frac{K_i z_i}{1 + V(K_i - 1)} . \tag{1.3-19}$$

Since the mole fractions must add up to unity, we have

$$\sum x_i = 1 \quad \text{and} \quad \sum y_i = 1.$$

Several different forms of functions may be used to describe flash vaporization. The one suggested by Rachford and Rice (1952) is preferable for computer solution. They use the relation

$$\sum y_i - \sum x_i = 0. \tag{1.3-20}$$

Substituting Eqs. (1.3-18) and (1.3-19) into (1.3-20),

$$F(V) = \sum \frac{z_i(K_i - 1)}{1 + V(K_i - 1)} = 0. \tag{1.3-21}$$

The problem of flash vaporization has now been reduced to that of finding the root of $F(V) = 0$. A plot of $F(V)$ vs. V, based on Eq. (1.3-21) is shown in Figure 1-6. The function is monotonically decreasing and has negative slopes. It is obvious that Newton's method applied to this case will always converge rapidly to the solution with any initial guess of V, $0 \leqslant V \leqslant 1$. For detailed discussions of convergence in flash calculations, see pp. 59-65, Holland (1975).

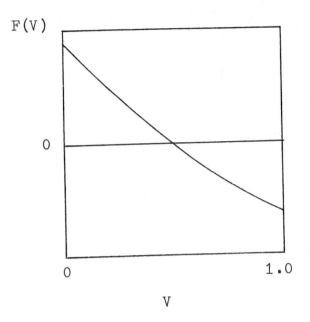

F(V)

0

0   1.0

V

Figure 1-6. A plot of F(V) vs. V based on the
Rachford-Rice equation

Before we start the computation, it is advisable to check
the necessary conditions for a flash to occur at a given
pressure. The flash temperature must be between the bubble
point and dew point temperatures, i.e.,

$$T_{b.p.} < T < T_{d.p.} .$$

(1.3-22)

We have derived the bubble point and dew point functions
in Examples 1.3-2 and 1.3-3.

$$F_1(T_{b.p.}) = \sum K_i x_i - 1 = 0,$$

$$F_2(T_{d.p.}) = \sum (y_i/K_i) - 1 = 0.$$

In order to satisfy   (1.3-22), we must have

$$\sum K_i z_i - 1 > 0,$$

$$\text{and} \quad \sum \frac{z_i}{K_i} - 1 > 0. \qquad \left.\begin{array}{c} \\ \\ \end{array}\right\} \qquad (1.3\text{-}23)$$

If (1.3-23) are satisfied, we can proceed to find V, the fraction vaporized, as follows:

(a) Make an initial guess of V. (Any value, $0 \leqslant V \leqslant 1$, may be used.)

(b) Compute $F(V) = \sum \dfrac{z_i (K_i - 1)}{1 + V(K_i - 1)}$

and $\quad F'(V) = -\sum \dfrac{z_i (K_i - 1)^2}{\left[1 + V(K_i - 1)\right]^2}$.

(c) Update V by Newton's method,

$$V_{new} = V_{old} - \frac{F(V_{old})}{F'(V_{old})}.$$

(d) Check for convergence. If $\left| F(V) \right| < \epsilon$, the fraction vaporized is found. If not, repeat steps (b) through (d).

PROGRAM FLASH

Description of Input/Output

N   -(input) the number of components

T   -(input) the temperature

P   -(input) the pressure

K   -(input) one-dimensional array containing the K-values

Table 1-11. PROGRAM FLASH

```
00100        PROGRAM FLASH(INPUT,OUTPUT)
00110        REAL K(10)
00120        DIMENSION X(10),Y(10),Z(10)
00130C
00140C       DATA INPUT
00150C
00160        READ*,N,T,P
00170        READ*,(K(I),I=1,N)
00180        READ*,(Z(I),I=1,N)
00190        READ*,V
00200C
00210C       CHECK BUBBLE POINT AND DEW POINT
00220C
00230        SUMX=0.    $SUMY=0.
00240        DO 20 I=1,N
00250        SUMX=SUMX+Z(I)/K(I)
00260     20 SUMY=SUMY+Z(I)*K(I)
00270        IF(SUMX.LT.1..OR.SUMY.LT.1.) GO TO 120
00280C
00290C       PRINT THE HEADING
00300C
00310        PRINT 30
00320     30 FORMAT(//5X,"THE VALUES OF V, FV, DFV, AND VNEW ARE"//)
00330C
00340C       SOLVING FRACTION VAPORIZED BY NEWTON'S METHOD
00350C
00360     40 FV=0.    $DFV=0.
00370        DO 50 I=1,N
00380        FV=FV+(K(I)-1.)*Z(I)/(1.-V+V*K(I))
00390     50 DFV=DFV-Z(I)*((K(I)-1.)/(1.-V+V*K(I)))**2
00400        VNEW=V-FV/DFV
00410        IF(ABS(FV).LT..1E-4) GO TO 70
00420        PRINT 60,V,FV,DFV,VNEW
00430     60 FORMAT(F8.4,2E15.5,F8.4)
00440        V=VNEW
00450        GO TO 40
00460C
00470C       PRINT ANSWERS
00480C
00490     70 PRINT 60,V,FV,DFV,VNEW
00500        PRINT 80,T,P
00510     80 FORMAT(//5X,"T =",F8.3," DEG F",5X,"P =", F8.2," ATM")
00520        DO 90 I=1,N
00530        X(I)=Z(I)/(1.-V+V*K(I))
00540     90 Y(I)=K(I)*X(I)
00550        PRINT 100,(Z(I),X(I),Y(I),K(I),I=1,N)
00560    100 FORMAT(//6X,"Z(I)",6X,"X(I)",6X,"Y(I)",6X,"K(I)"//
00570+        (4F10.4))
00580        PRINT 110,V
00590    110 FORMAT(//10X,"FRACTION VAPORIZED =",F7.4)
00600        GO TO 140
00610    120 PRINT 130
00620    130 FORMAT(//10X,"THERE IS NO SOLUTION.")
00630    140 STOP
00640        END
```

30

Table 1-12. An application of PROGRAM FLASH
DATA INPUT AT TIME OF EXECUTION

? 3, 260., 1.
? 4.6431, 1.0328, .2517   — K_i
? .4, .3, .3
? .5
OUTPUT

        THE VALUES OF V, FV, DFV, AND VNEW ARE

    .5000   .16745E+00   -.10960E+01   .6528
    .6528   .21420E-02   -.11075E+01   .6547
    .6547   -.16502E-05   -.11092E+01   .6547

    T = 260.000 DEG F   P =   1.00 ATM

    Z(I)   X(I)   Y(I)   K(I)

    .4000   .1182   .5486   4.6431
    .3000   .2937   .3033   1.0328
    .3000   .5881   .1480   .2517

        FRACTION VAPORIZED =   .6547

31

Z   -(input) one-dimensional array containing the mole
        fractions of components in the feed

V   -(input) initial guess of the fraction vaporized

FV   -(intermediate calculations) a function of V based on the
        Rachford-Rice equation

DFV   -(intermediate calculations) the first derivative of FV

V   -(output) converged solution of fraction vaporized

X   -(output) one-dimensional array containing the mole
        fractions of components in the liquid

Y   -(output) one-dimensional array containing the mole
        fractions of components in the vapor

$\frown$ p.30

PROGRAM FLASH (see Table 1-11) was run with an initially

guessed value of V = 0.5. The convergence criterion was

$|F(V)| < \epsilon$. The tolerance limit was set at $\epsilon = 1.0 \times 10^{-5}$.

After three iterations the solution was

Fraction vaporized = 0.6547.

The compositions of the liquid and vapor products were

x_i	y_i
.1182	.5486
.2937	.3033
.5881	.1480

The computer printout was given in Table 1-12.

1.4   The Method of Regula Falsi

The method of regula falsi is initiated by selecting two

estimates of the root, say x_1 and x_2. We proceed to find a new and improved estimate of x such that $f(x) = 0$.

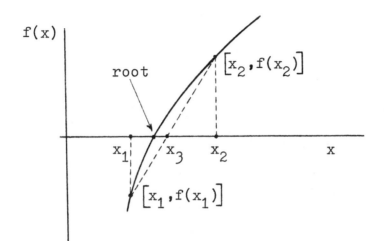

Figure 1-7. Root determination by the
method of regula falsi

It is obtained by connecting a straight line between points $\left[x_1, \ f(x_1)\right]$ and $\left[x_2, \ f(x_2)\right]$ in Figure 1-7. The x-intercept is designated x_3. The equation of a straight line passing through the two given points is

$$\frac{f(x) - f(x_1)}{x - x_1} = \frac{f(x) - f(x_2)}{x - x_2} \, . \tag{1.4-1}$$

Since we intend to have $f(x) = 0$ at $x = x_3$, we have

$$\frac{0 - f(x_1)}{x_3 - x_1} = \frac{0 - f(x_2)}{x_3 - x_2} \, . \tag{1.4-2}$$

Rearranging,

33

$$x_3 = \frac{x_1 f(x_2) - x_2 f(x_1)}{f(x_2) - f(x_1)} . \tag{1.4-3}$$

Or, in general,

$$x_{n+2} = \frac{x_n f(x_{n+1}) - x_{n+1} f(x_n)}{f(x_{n+1}) - f(x_n)} . \tag{1.4-4}$$

Again, there is no guarantee that this method will converge to the desired solution. The following general procedure may be used.

(a) Make an initial guess of $x = x_1$ and evaluate $f(x_1)$.

(b) Make a second guess of $x = x_2$ and evaluate $f(x_2)$.

(c) A new, and hopefully improved, estimate of x is given by Eq. (1.4-4). Always use the results of the two latest estimates to obtain the new estimate. (Note that sometimes the new estimate could fall outside the interval x_2 -- x_1 of the first and second guesses.)

(d) Convergence check. If $|f(x)| < \epsilon$, the solution is at hand. If not, repeat steps (c) and (d). The choice of ϵ depends on the circumstances.

EXAMPLE 1.4-1. Multiple-stage Countercurrent Extraction

In a 3-stage countercurrent extraction, the feed containing a mixture of A and C is extracted with a pure solvent B. Components A and B are immiscible, while component C transfers from the feed stream to the solvent stream. The feed concentration of 0.1 g-mole of C per liter is eventually reduced to

34

0.05 g-mole/L in the final raffinate. Since solute C is relatively dilute, we can assume that the flow rates of the two phases are essentially constant.

The feed is introduced at a rate of 300 L/h. The equilibrium relations may be represented by

$$y = 2.5 \; x^{1.194},$$

where y = concentration of solute C in the extract phase, g-mole/L,

x = concentration of solute C in the raffinate phase, g-mole/L.

Determine the necessary solvent rate for the specified separation.

A flow diagram of the countercurrent extraction process is given in Figure 1-8.

Extract phase flow rate = B

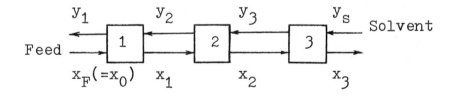

Raffinate phase flow rate = A

Figure 1-8. A three-stage countercurrent extractor

Material balance of solute C around stage 3 gives

$$Ax_2 + By_s = Ax_3 + By_3. \qquad (1.4-5)$$

For a pure solvent, $y_s = 0$. Rearranging,

$$y_3 = \frac{A}{B} x_2 - \frac{A}{B} x_3. \qquad (1.4-6)$$

Similarly, material balances around stages 2 and 3, and around stages 1, 2, and 3 yield, respectively,

$$y_2 = \frac{A}{B} x_1 - \frac{A}{B} x_3, \qquad (1.4-7)$$

$$y_1 = \frac{A}{B} x_0 - \frac{A}{B} x_3. \qquad (1.4-8)$$

In general, the material balances can be represented by an equation of the form

$$y_m = \frac{A}{B} x_{m-1} - \frac{A}{B} x_n$$

or

$$x_{m-1} = \frac{B}{A} y_m + x_n. \qquad (1.4-9)$$

The problem can also be solved graphically on a McCabe-Thiele diagram. See Figure 1-9.

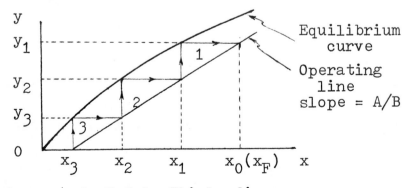

Figure 1-9. McCabe-Thiele diagram

The material balance equations are represented by a straight line, the operating line, with a slope of A/B, passing through the point $(x_3, 0)$. The stepwise construction on the McCabe-Thiele diagram is accomplished by alternately drawing vertical and horizontal lines between the equilibrium curve and the operating line.

$$x_3 \rightarrow y_3 \rightarrow x_2 \rightarrow y_2 \rightarrow x_1 \rightarrow y_1 \rightarrow x_0 (x_F) \qquad (1.4\text{-}10)$$

Each step represents an extracting stage.

The graphical method described above can help us to understand how the extraction problem is solved analytically. In a stagewise calculation we proceed to attack the problem by solving the material balance equation and the equilibrium relationship, alternately. The stepping-off procedure on the McCabe-Thiele diagram accomplishes just the same, graphically.

In the given problem, the number of stages n, the feed rate A, the feed composition x_F, and the raffinate composition x_n are specified. It is required to find the solvent rate B. This must be a trial-and-error solution. Computers are well adapted to handle this kind of problem.

We start by estimating the value of B, which is equivalent to fixing the slope of the operating line on the McCabe-Thiele diagram. Stagewise calculations following the sequence of (1.4-10) will end up at x_0. If $x_0 = x_F$, the estimated value of B is correct. If not, the difference, $x_F - x_0$, which is a

function of B, can be used as a means to improve the estimate.
Our purpose is to find a value of B such that $x_F - x_O = 0$.
In other words, the extraction problem has been reduced to
that of finding the root of a certain function of B. The method
of regula falsi requires two initially selected values of B,
from which the corresponding values of the function are computed.
We arbitrarily set the second guess of B as 1.1 times the first
guess. Thence the interpolation formula, Eq. (1.4-4), is used
to obtain a new and improved estimate of B, until $|x_F - x_O| < \epsilon$.
The tolerance limit ϵ is set at 1.0×10^{-5}.

PROGRAM EXTN1

Description of Input/Output

N   -(input) the number of equilibrium stages

XF   -(input) the feed composition

XN   -(input) the raffinate composition

A   -(input) the flow rate of the feed

B   -(input) the flow rate of the solvent, initially an
         estimated value

EPS   -(input) the tolerance limit

B   -(output) the flow rate of the solvent (converged
         solution)

X   -(output) one-dimensional array containing the concen-
         trations of the solute in the raffinate phase

Y   -(output) one-dimensional array containing the concen-
         trations of the solute in the extract phase

Table 1-13. PROGRAM EXTN1

```
00100        PROGRAM EXTN1(INPUT,OUTPUT)
00110        DIMENSION X(10),Y(10)
00120C
00130C       DATA INPUT
00140C
00150        READ*,N,XF,XN,A,B,EPS
00160C
00170C       PRINT HEADING
00180C
00190        PRINT 5
00200      5 FORMAT(//5X,"TRIAL-AND-ERROR SOLUTION",//
00210+       16X,"ITER",9X,"B",8X,"X0",/)
00220C
00230C       METHOD OF REGULA FALSI
00240C
00250        ITER=0
00260C
00270C       FIRST GUESS OF B
00280C
00290        B1=B    $X(N)=XN
00300     10 DO 20 J=1,N
00310        K=N-J+1
00320        Y(K)=2.5*X(K)**1.194
00330        IF(K.EQ.1) GO TO 30
00340        X(K-1)=B/A*Y(K)+XN
00350     20 CONTINUE
00360     30 ITER=ITER+1
00370        X0=B/A*Y(1)+XN
00380        PRINT 35,ITER,B,X0
00390     35 FORMAT(10X,I10,F10.2,F10.5)
00400        IF(ITER.GE.2) GO TO 40
00410        FUNC1=XF-X0
00420C
00430C       SECOND GUESS OF B IS ARBITRARILY TAKEN AS 1.1 TIMES
00440C       OF THE FIRST GUESS.
00450C
00460        B=1.1*B    $B2=B    $GO TO 10
00470     40 FUNC2=XF-X0
00480C
00490C       CHECK CONVERGENCE
00500C
00510        IF(ABS(FUNC2).LT.EPS) GO TO 50
00520C
00530C       UPDATE B AND MAKE ANOTHER TRY.
00540C
00550        B=(B1*FUNC2-B2*FUNC1)/(FUNC2-FUNC1)
00560        B1=B2    $B2=B    $FUNC1=FUNC2    $GO TO 10
00570C
00580C       CONVERGENCE ACHIEVED - PRINT FINAL RESULTS.
00590C
00600     50 PRINT 55
00610     55 FORMAT(//5X,"FINAL RESULTS",//)
00620        PRINT 60,XF,XN,N,A,B
00630     60 FORMAT(//8X,"XF",8X,"XN",9X,"N",9X,"A",9X,"B",
00640+       //2F10.5,I10,2F10.2)
00650        PRINT 70,(I,X(I),Y(I),I=1,N)
00660     70 FORMAT(//9X,"I",6X,"X(I)",6X,"Y(I)"/(I10,2F10.5))
00670        STOP
00680        END
```

39

Table 1-14. An application of PROGRAM EXTN1

DATA INPUT AT TIME OF EXECUTION

? 3, .1, .05, 300., 100., 1.E-5

OUTPUT

TRIAL-AND-ERROR SOLUTION

ITER	B	XO
1	100.00	.09502
2	110.00	.10309
3	106.17	.09990
4	106.29	.10000

FINAL RESULTS

XF	XN	N	A	B
.10000	.05000	3	300.00	106.29

I	X(I)	Y(I)
1	.09004	.14111
2	.07477	.11302
3	.05000	.06991

PROGRAM EXTN1 (see Table 1-13) was developed to solve Example 1.4-1 by the method of regula falsi. Notice that we had included more than one statement on line 00290, 00460, and 00560. The symbol $ was used to separate each statement. We used an initial guess of B = 100. The tolerance limit was ϵ = 0.00001. After four iterations the solution was

$$B = 106.29 \text{ L/h.}$$

The computer printout (see Table 1-14) also gave solute concentrations in various stages:

Stage	x_i	y_i
1	.09004	.14111
2	.07477	.11302
3	.05000	.06991

EXAMPLE 1.4-2. Multiple-stage Crosscurrent Extraction

Rework Example 1.4-1 for a 3-stage crosscurrent extraction, with an equal amount of fresh solvent supplied to each stage.

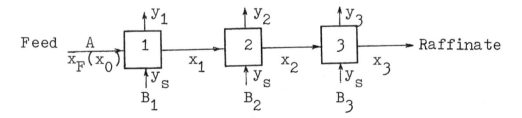

Flow rate of feed stream = A
Flow rate of solvent stream: $B_1 = B_2 = B_3 = B$

Figure 1-10. A three-stage crosscurrent extractor

The flow diagram of a 3-stage crosscurrent extractor is shown in Figure 1-10. We perform a material balance of the solute around stage 1 to obtain

$$Ax_0 + By_s = Ax_1 + By_1. \qquad (1.4\text{-}11)$$

Setting $y_s = 0$ for pure solvent and rearranging,

$$y_1 = -\frac{A}{B}x_1 + \frac{A}{B}x_0. \qquad (1.4\text{-}12)$$

Similarly, material balances around stages 2 and 3 yield, respectively,

$$y_2 = -\frac{A}{B}x_2 + \frac{A}{B}x_1, \qquad (1.4\text{-}13)$$

$$y_3 = -\frac{A}{B}x_3 + \frac{A}{B}x_2. \qquad (1.4\text{-}14)$$

In general,

$$y_m = -\frac{A}{B}x_m + \frac{A}{B}x_{m-1} \qquad (1.4\text{-}15)$$

or

$$x_{m-1} = \frac{B}{A}y_m + x_m. \qquad (1.4\text{-}16)$$

The problem can be solved graphically as shown in Figure 1-11, where the material balance equations are represented by operating lines with slope $-\frac{A}{B}$.

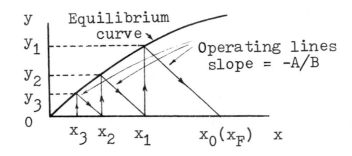

Figure 1-11. Graphical solution of 3-stage crosscurrent extraction

We start from x_3 on the abscissa, connecting a vertical line to the equilibrium curve to find y_3. From there we draw an operating line of slope $-\frac{A}{B}$ to find x_2 on the abscissa. This process of using the equilibrium curve and the operating line alternately is continued until we reach $x_0(x_F)$.

$$x_3 \rightarrow y_3 \rightarrow x_2 \rightarrow y_2 \rightarrow x_1 \rightarrow y_1 \rightarrow x_0(x_F)$$

The given problem must be solved by a trial-and-error method. We start by estimating the value of B and carry on the stagewise calculations to obtain x_0. The difference, $x_F - x_0$, is used to improve the estimate. The method of regula falsi requires two initially selected values of B. Our second guess is programed as 1.1 times the first guess. After that, the interpolation formula of Eq. (1.4-4) takes over until the converged solution is found.

PROGRAM EXTN2 (see Table 1-15) is a FORTRAN IV program that was developed to solve the crosscurrent extraction problem of Example 1.4-2 by the method of regula falsi. Notice that we had entered more than one statement on line 00290, 00460, and 00560. The symbol $ was used to separate one statement from another.

PROGRAM EXTN2

Description of Input/Output

N   -(input) the number of equilibrium extraction stages

XF   -(input) the feed composition

XN   -(input) the raffinate composition

A   -(input) the flow rate of the feed

B   -(input) the estimated flow rate of solvent to each stage

EPS   -(input) the tolerance limit

B   -(output) the flow rate of solvent to each stage
        (converged solution)

BTOTAL-(output) total amount of solvent = B x N

X   -(output) one-dimensional array containing the concen-
        tration of the solute in the raffinate phase

Y   -(output) one-dimensional array containing the concen-
        tration of the solute in the extract phase

PROGRAM EXTN2 (see Table 1-15) was run to solve Example
1.4-2. The initial guess was B = 40 and the tolerance limit
was ϵ = 1.0 x 10^{-5}. After five iterations the solution was
B = 53.36 L/h. The total amount of solvent required for three
stages was BTOTAL = 160.09 L/h. The computer printout (see
Table 1-16) also gave the following concentrations of solute
in various stages:

Stage	x_i	y_i
1	.07865	.12005
2	.06243	.09113
3	.05000	.06991

We find in the previous example that for the same separation in a 3-stage countercurrent extractor the solvent required
is only 106.29 L/h, which is considerably less than that

Table 1-15. PROGRAM EXTN2

```
00100          PROGRAM EXTN2(INPUT,OUTPUT)
00110          DIMENSION X(10),Y(10)
00120C
00130C         DATA INPUT
00140C
00150          READ*,N,XF,XN,A,B,EPS
00160C
00170C         PRINT HEADING
00180C
00190          PRINT 5
00200       5 FORMAT(//5X,"TRIAL-AND-ERROR SOLUTION",//
00210+         16X,"ITER",9X,"B",8X,"X0",/)
00220C
00230C         METHOD OF REGULA FALSI
00240C
00250          ITER=0
00260C
00270C         FIRST GUESS OF B
00280C
00290          B1=B    $X(N)=XN
00300      10 DO 20 J=1,N
00310          K=N-J+1
00320          Y(K)=2.5*X(K)**1.194
00330          IF(K.EQ.1) GO TO 30
00340          X(K-1)=B/A*Y(K)+X(K)
00350      20 CONTINUE
00360      30 ITER=ITER+1
00370          X0=B/A*Y(1)+X(1)
00380          PRINT 35,ITER,B,X0
00390      35 FORMAT(10X,I10,F10.2,F10.5)
00400          IF(ITER.GE.2) GO TO 40
00410          FUNC1=XF-X0
00420C
00430C         SECOND GUESS OF B IS ARBITRARILY TAKEN AS 1.1 TIMES
00440C         OF THE FIRST GUESS.
00450C
00460          B=1.1*B    $B2=B    $GO TO 10
00470      40 FUNC2=XF-X0
00480C
00490C         CHECK CONVERGENCE
00500C
00510          IF(ABS(FUNC2).LT.EPS) GO TO 50
00520C
00530C         UPDATE B AND MAKE ANOTHER TRY.
00540C
00550          B=(B1*FUNC2-B2*FUNC1)/(FUNC2-FUNC1)
00560          B1=B2    $B2=B    $FUNC1=FUNC2    $GO TO 10
00570C
00580C         CONVERGENCE ACHIEVED - PRINT FINAL RESULTS.
00590C
00600      50 PRINT 55
00610      55 FORMAT(//5X,"FINAL RESULTS",//)
00620          BTOTAL=B*N
00630          PRINT 60,XF,XN,N,A,B,BTOTAL
00635      60 FORMAT(//8X,"XF",8X,"XN",9X,"N",9X,"A",9X,"B",
00640+         4X,"BTOTAL"//2F10.5,I10,3F10.2)
00650          PRINT 70,(I,X(I),Y(I),I=1,N)
00660      70 FORMAT(//9X,"I",6X,"X(I)",6X,"Y(I)"/(I10,2F10.5))
00670          STOP
00680          END
```

Table 1-16. An application of PROGRAM EXTN2

DATA INPUT AT TIME OF EXECUTION

? 3, .1, .05, 300., 40., 1.E-5

OUTPUT

TRIAL-AND-ERROR SOLUTION

ITER	B	XO
1	40.00	.08486
2	44.00	.08919
3	53.99	.10076
4	53.34	.09997
5	53.36	.10000

FINAL RESULTS

XF	XN	N	A	B	BTOTAL
.10000	.05000	3	300.00	53.36	160.09

I	X(I)	Y(I)
1	.07865	.12005
2	.06243	.09113
3	.05000	.06991

required in the 3-stage crosscurrent extractor. While one example does not necessarily prove that the countercurrent operation is more efficient, it is well known to practising chemical engineers that very often the countercurrent principle can be used to our advantage.

1.5 The Muller's Method

The Muller's method (1956) is widely used for finding roots of functions. It starts with three initially picked points, x_1, x_2, and x_3. The corresponding values of the functions are $f(x_1)$, $f(x_2)$, and $f(x_3)$. It is assumed that the function can be approximated by a parabola passing through these points. The equation of this parabola is

$$f(x) = ax^2 + bx + c. \qquad (1.5-1)$$

The coefficients a, b, and c in Eq. (1.5-1) are given by the following equations:

$$\left.\begin{aligned} a &= d_1 + d_2 + d_3, \\ b &= -\left[(x_2+x_3)d_1 + (x_3+x_1)d_2 + (x_1+x_2)d_3\right], \\ c &= x_2x_3d_1 + x_3x_1d_2 + x_1x_2d_3, \end{aligned}\right\} \qquad (1.5-2)$$

where

$$\left.\begin{aligned} d_1 &= -\frac{f(x_1)}{(x_3-x_1)(x_1-x_2)}, \\[2mm] d_2 &= -\frac{f(x_2)}{(x_1-x_2)(x_2-x_3)}, \end{aligned}\right\} \qquad (1.5-3)$$

47

$$d_3 = - \frac{f(x_3)}{(x_2 - x_3)(x_3 - x_1)} \cdot \Bigg\}$$

Once a, b, and c are calculated from Eqs. (1.5-2) and (1.5-3), a fourth point is found by setting f(x) of Eq. (1.5-1) equal to zero and solving for x,

$$x_4 = \frac{- b \pm \sqrt{b^2 - 4ac}}{2a}. \qquad (1.5-4)$$

The sign in Eq. (1.5-4) is chosen such that x_4 will be as close to x_3 as possible. x_4 is an approximation of the root.

The oldest point, x_1, is then discarded. The above method is applied again, using the latest three points, $\left[x_2, \ f(x_2)\right]$, $\left[x_3, \ f(x_3)\right]$, and $\left[x_4, \ f(x_4)\right]$. Notice that in computer programming the three points are renamed x_1, x_2, and x_3, respectively. The procedure is repeated until $|x_4 - x_3| < \epsilon$.

EXAMPLE 1.5-1. The Muller's Method

Rework Example 1.3-2, finding the bubble-point temperature by Muller's method.

PROGRAM BBLTM

Description of Input/Output

N   -(input) the number of components

X   -(input) one-dimensional array containing the liquid
        mole fractions

A,B,C -(input) one-dimensional arrays containing the coeffi-
    cients of the K-value equation

T   -(input) the initial estimate of the bubble-point
    temperature

T1,T2,T3 -(intermediate calculation) the three points to
    initiate the Muller's method

F1,F2,F3 -(intermediate calculation) the corresponding function-
    al values at T1, T2, and T3, respectively

T4   -(output) the bubble-point temperature

F4   -(output) the functional value at T4

Y   -(output) one-dimensional array containing the vapor
    mole fractions in equilibrium with the liquid

K   -(output) one-dimensional array containing the K-values
    at the bubble-point temperature

Solution of the bubble-point temperature by Muller's

method was first reported in literature by Wang and Henke (1966).

A computer solution using PROGRAM BBLTM (see Table 1-17) is

presented here. The program follows closely what has been

discussed under Sec. 1.5. Notice that in the program we have

included more than one statement on one line. The symbol $ is

used to separate each statement.

The initial estimate of the temperature is read in as an

input.(We used T = 200.)   Since Muller's method requires three

initial points, we arbitrarily assign the other two T - 10

and T + 10, respectively. The values of the function at the

given temperatures are calculated, using a subprogram, FUNCTION

F(T), which follows Eqs. (1.3-6) and (1.3-7). The main program

49

Table 1-17. PROGRAM BBLTM

```
00100        PROGRAM BBLTM(INPUT,OUTPUT)
00110        REAL K
00120        COMMON N,A(10),B(10),C(10),X(10),Y(10),K(10)
00130C
00140C       DATA INPUT
00150C
00160        READ*,N
00165        READ*,(X(I),I=1,N)
00170        READ*,(A(I),B(I),C(I),I=1,N)
00180        READ*,T
00190C
00200C       EVALUATE VALUES OF FUNCTION AT THREE GIVEN POINTS.
00210C
00220        T1=T-10.   $T2=T   $T3=T+10.
00230        F1=F(T1)   $F2=F(T2)   $F3=F(T3)
00240        PRINT 5,T1,F1,T2,F2,T3,F3
00250      5 FORMAT(//5X,"INITIAL VALUES USED TO START ITERATION"/
00260+       6X,"T",9X,"F(T)"/(F10.2,E16.8))
00270C
00280C       THE MULLER'S METHOD
00290C
00300        PRINT 6
00310      6 FORMAT(//5X,"RESULT OF MULLER'S METHOD"/
00320+       6X,"T",9X,"F(T)")
00330     10 CALL MULLER(T1,T2,T3,T4,F1,F2,F3)
00340        F4=F(T4)
00350        IF(ABS(T4-T3).LT..01) GO TO 30
00360C
00370C       USE THE LATEST THREE POINTS TO MAKE ANOTHER ITERATION.
00380C
00390        T1=T2   $T2=T3   $T3=T4
00400        F1=F2   $F2=F3   $F3=F4
00410C
00420C       OUTPUT
00430C
00440        PRINT 25,T4,F4
00450     25 FORMAT(F10.2,E16.8)
00460        GO TO 10
00470     30 DO 40 I=1,N
00480     40 Y(I)=K(I)*X(I)
00490        PRINT 50,T4
00500     50 FORMAT(//5X,"BUBBLE POINT TEMPERATURE =",F10.2)
00510        PRINT 60,(X(I),Y(I),K(I),I=1,N)
00520     60 FORMAT(//5X,"X(I)",6X,"Y(I)",6X,"K(I)"//(3F10.4))
00530        STOP
00540        END
```

```
00580        FUNCTION F(T)
00590        REAL K
00600        COMMON N,A(10),B(10),C(10),X(10),Y(10),K(10)
00610        SUM=-1.
00620        DO 10 I=1,N
00630        K(I)=EXP(A(I)+B(I)*T+C(I)*T*T)
00640     10 SUM=SUM+K(I)*X(I)
00650        F=SUM
00660        RETURN
00670        END
```

```
00710        SUBROUTINE MULLER(X1,X2,X3,X4,F1,F2,F3)
00720        D1=-F1/((X3-X1)*(X1-X2))
00730        D2=-F2/((X1-X2)*(X2-X3))
00740        D3=-F3/((X2-X3)*(X3-X1))
00750        A=D1+D2+D3
00760        B=-((X2+X3)*D1+(X3+X1)*D2+(X1+X2)*D3)
00770        C=X2*X3*D1+X3*X1*D2+X1*X2*D3
00780        IF(A.EQ.0.) X4=-C/B
00790        IF(A.EQ.0.) GO TO 10
00800        DISCR=B*B-4.*A*C
00810        IF(DISCR.LE.0.) X4=-B/(2.*A)
00820        IF(DISCR.LE.0.) GO TO 10
00830        X4=(-B+SQRT(DISCR))/(2.*A)
00840        XX=(-B-SQRT(DISCR))/(2.*A)
00850        IF(ABS(XX-X3).LT.ABS(X4-X3)) X4=XX
00860     10 RETURN
00870        END
```

Table 1-18. An application of PROGRAM BBLTM
DATA INPUT AT TIME OF EXECUTION

? 3
? .1104, .2829, .6067
? -2.99279, 2.2270E-2, -1.8669E-5
? -5.90449, 2.9968E-2, -2.7439E-5
? -8.72046, 3.7367E-2, -3.5124E-5
? 200.

OUTPUT
        INITIAL VALUES USED TO START ITERATION
        T   F(T)
     190.00   -.68696821E+00
     200.00   -.62847090E+00
     210.00   -.56068697E+00

        RESULT OF MULLER'S METHOD
        T   F(T)
     266.76   .55544213E-01
     262.82   -.25758525E-02
     262.99   -.68566289E-05

     BUBBLE POINT TEMPERATURE =   262.99

     X(I)   Y(I)   K(I)

     .1104   .5322   4.8203
     .2829   .3062   1.0823
     .6067   .1617   .2665

then calls SUBROUTINE MULLER to find T4, which is the approximation of the root. The algorithm used in SUBROUTINE MULLER is based on Eqs. (1.5-2), (1.5-3), and (1.5-4). The convergence criterion is $|T4 - T3| < \epsilon$. ϵ is arbitrarily assigned 0.01.

The computer printout is given in Table 1-18. The solution, the bubble-point temperature = 262.99°F, is the same as that of Example 1.3-2.

1.6 Comparison of Methods

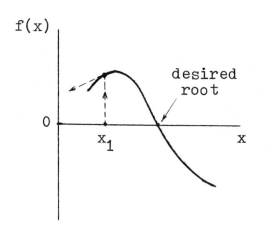

Figure 1-12(a)

A case of no convergence in Newton's method

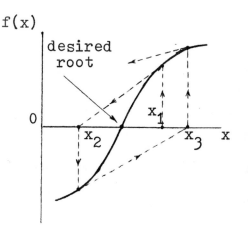

Figure 1-12(b)

Another case of no convergence in Newton's method

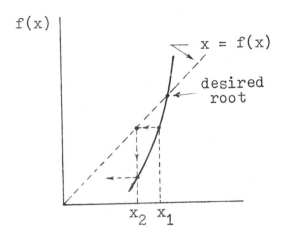 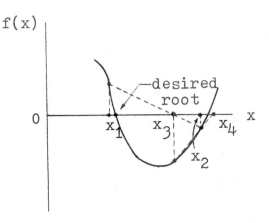

Figure 1-12(c)

A case when the method
of successive substitutions
diverges

Figure 1-12(d)

A case when the method
of regula falsi fails
to converge to the
desired root

It is difficult to single out which method is the best.
Newton's method is popular, because it is simple to use and
generally converges rapidly. It does have certain limitations.
With a bad initial guess, Newton's method may not converge to
the desired root, as illustrated in Figure 1-12(a). A second
case in which Newton's method may never converge is illustrated
in Figure 1-12(b), when there is a point of inflection. Besides,
if the function has a maximum or minimum where the first derivative is equal to zero, Newton's method might run into the
trouble of division by zero. We should also note that sometimes
the evaluation of the first derivative by an analytical method
could be difficult or impossible, because the function itself

might not be expressible in a simple analytical form. An alternative is to evaluate the first derivative by an approximation formula as described in Sec. 4.4.

Fortunately, there are other methods available to overcome some of the limitations encountered in Newton's method. Both the method of successive substitutions and the method of regula falsi do not involve the derivatives of the function. They have their own limitations, though. The method of successive substitutions requires that the function be rearranged explicitly in the form x = f(x), which is not always possible. The method usually converges more slowly, if it does converge. The illustration in Figure 1-12(c) shows that the method may diverge when the slope of the function in the neighborhood of the desired root is greater than 1. The method of regula falsi needs two initially selected values of x, therefore, more programming. It is to be observed that the method may fail to converge to the desired root when the function has several roots in an interval, as shown in Figure 1-12(d).

The bisection method is reliable since it always converges. The limitations are that the interval containing the desired root must be established first and that there is one and only one root in that interval. The rate of convergence is relatively slow.

The Muller's method is essentially a method of quadratic interpolation, and converges faster than Newton's method, which

uses a linear interpolation. Since the Muller's method uses
three selected values of x to approximate the function by a
parabola, the calculation per iteration is longer. It does not
necessarily save computer time as compared with Newton's method.
The advantage of the Muller's method is the greater likelihood
of success for convergence.

There are numerous books which give methods for the
solution of nonlinear equations. The text by Gerald (1970)
provides simple treatments. Hornbeck (1975) and Williams (1973)
present general descriptions of methods and examples where
difficulties arise. Standard texts, such as McCracken and Dorn
(1964), Dorn and McCracken (1972), and Conte and de Boor (1980),
contain descriptions of methods together with computer programs
and worked examples. Carnahan, Luther, and Wilkes (1969)
discuss various numerical methods and illustrate them by
programs, many of which are related to applications in engineering. More extensive treatments are provided by Hildebrand (1974),
Scarborough (1966), Ralston and Rabinowitz (1978), Traub (1964),
and Forsythe, Malcolm, and Moler (1977). Hamming (1973) and
Wilkinson (1964) devote special attention to errors.

APPENDIX

Methods of Terminating an Iterative Procedure

To find a root of the function $f(x)$ is to choose a value x_n such that $f(x_n) = 0$. The numerical solution usually uses an iterative procedure to successively adjust the value of x until a desired result is obtained. In most cases $f(x_n)$ will not be exactly zero, but will be made as close to zero as desired. In other words, we must set beforehand a "stop criterion" (or criteria) to terminate the iteration when our goal is achieved. We will discuss the most commonly used techniques.

(1) The direct method -- $\left| f(x_n) \right| < \epsilon$, where ϵ is a small positive number. At first the method looks straightforward; however, if ϵ is too small, the calculation will require excessive computer time while the adjustment in the final answer is insignificant. On the other hand, if ϵ is not small enough, the program will be prematurely terminated before the right answer is obtained, assuming that the program does converge. Since we do not know the answer, it is difficult to assign the value of ϵ at the very beginning.

(2) The ratio method -- $\left| 1 - \frac{x_{n+1}}{x_n} \right| < \epsilon$. For most engineering applications, $\epsilon = .001$ will be satisfactory. This implies that the program will be stopped when the values of x obtained

in two successive iterations differ from each other by less than one thousandth part of x_n. The disadvantage is that the method fails when zero is the root.

(3) the difference method -- $|x_{n+1} - x_n| < \epsilon$. Method (3) can be used to avoid the pitfall of dividing by zero in method (2). The difference method is more or less equivalent to arbitrarily specifying the accuracy. For instance, in Examples 1.3-2 and 1.3-3, we seldom require the bubble-point or dew-point temperature to be accurate within $\pm.01$ degree. Thus it is reasonably safe to choose $\epsilon = .01$.

(4) Maximum number of iterations -- The program is stopped after a specified number of iterations. For example, in PROGRAN BISECT we arbitrarily set 20 as the maximum number of iterations. At the end, the interval is reduced to $1/2^{20}$ of the original, and the midpoint of the final interval is a good approximation of the root. Also, if the program may diverge, it should be stopped when the search is unsu essful. Examples are step (d) of Sec. 1.2 and Sec. 1.3.

(5) Transfer of control -- If certain things happen, the program is stopped by transferring control to a STOP statement or by printing a message before STOP. An example is line 00440 of PROGRAM VIRIAL1.

PROBLEMS

1-A. In the analysis of a certain chemical reaction, a student
has arrived at the following equation:

$$f(x) = \frac{x(2.75 - x)}{(1.5 - x)^{1.5}(1 - x)^{0.5}} - 1.575 = 0, \qquad (1.A-1)$$

where x = extent of the reaction. ($0 < x < 1$.   x = 0 means no
    reaction; x = 1 means complete reaction.)

Write a computer program to find the value of x which satisfies
Eq. (1.A-1).   Solve by the method of bisection.

Answer: .4975

1-B. For turbulent flow in pipes, the friction factor is given
by the Moody chart (1944), which is based on the following
equation:

$$\frac{1}{\sqrt{f}} = -4 \log_{10} \left(\frac{\epsilon}{3.7D} + \frac{1.255}{Re \sqrt{f}} \right), \qquad (1.B-1)$$

where D = pipe diameter (m),

    f = friction factor,

    Re = Reynolds number,

    ϵ = pipe roughness (m).

Eq. (1.B-1) is implicit in f.   It is solved iteratively as
follows:

Letting $y = \dfrac{1}{4\sqrt{f}}$ (1.B-2) and substituting Eq. (1.B-2) into (1.B-1), we obtain

$$y = - \log_{10} \left(\frac{\epsilon}{3.7D} + \frac{5.02y}{Re} \right). \qquad (1.B-3)$$

Eq. (1.B-3) is now in the proper form to be solved by the method of successive substitutions. If we choose a starting value of y close to the solution, fast convergence will be ensured. The value of f can then be obtained from Eq. (1.B-2).

Recently Pham (1979) has derived the following explicit equation for turbulent pipe flow:

$$\frac{1}{\sqrt{f}} = -4 \log_{10} \left[\frac{\epsilon}{3.7D} - \frac{4.52}{Re} \log_{10} \left(\frac{7}{Re} + \frac{\epsilon}{7D} \right) \right], \qquad (1.B-4)$$

$$\text{or} \qquad y = - \log_{10} \left[\frac{\epsilon}{3.7D} - \frac{4.52}{Re} \log_{10} \left(\frac{7}{Re} + \frac{\epsilon}{7D} \right) \right]. \qquad (1.B-5)$$

You are asked to check the accuracy of Pham's equation. So prepare a computer program to solve Eq. (1.B-3) by the method of successive substitutions. For starting values of y you may use Eq. (1.B-5). The computer program reads in values of ϵ/D and Re and computes f which satisfies Eq. (1.B-1). The ranges of the parameters are

$$\epsilon/D = 0 \; -- \; .05,$$
$$Re = 3 \times 10^3 \; -- \; 1 \times 10^8.$$

For purpose of comparison, the output should print out the values of f from Eq. (1.B-1) and the corresponding values from Eq. (1.B-4).

Sample answers: At ϵ/D = .001 and Re = 1 x 10^5

f = .005544 from Eq. (1.B-1)

f = .005535 from Eq. (1.B-4)

1-C. The Redlich-Kwong (1949) equation of state is widely used
for engineering calculation of P-V-T relations of gases.

$$\left[P + \frac{a}{T^{0.5} V(V + b)} \right] (V - b) = RT, \qquad (1.C-1)$$

where P = pressure (atm),

   T = temperature (^{O}K),

   V = specific volume (liter/g-mole),

   R = gas constant = .082057 liter-atm/(g-mole-^{O}K),

   a, b = Redlich-Kwong constants.

Write a computer program to find the specific volume of a gas
at a given temperature and pressure by use of the Redlich-
Kwong equation. Solve Eq. (1.C-1) by the method of regula
falsi. To test the validity of your program, you will run the
program to evaluate the specific volume of carbon dioxide at
50 atm and 373.15^{O}K. The Redlich-Kwong constants for carbon
dioxide are

$$a = 63.726 \text{ atm-}(^{O}K)^{0.5}\text{-liter}^2/(g\text{-mole})^2,$$

$$b = 0.02967 \text{ liter/g-mole}.$$

(Suggestions: Solution of the Redlich-Kwong equation by the
method of regula falsi needs two initial guesses of V. The
first guess may be obtained from the ideal gas equation,

61

V = RT/P. The second guess may be taken as 1.1 times the first guess.)

Answer: .531 L/g-mole

1-D. In the Löschmidt experiment to measure the mutual diffusivity of a gas pair, two gases A and B are initially confined in a cylinder separated by a partition which divides the cylinder into two sections of equal volume. The pressure and temperature of the system are kept constant. When the partition is withdrawn for a definite time, there is interdiffusion of the gases. The partition is then replaced, and the contents of each half are allowed to mix. Then the contents are analyzed.

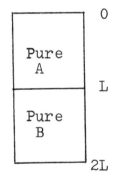

Figure P1-D. Löschmidt diffusion cell

Theoretically, the difference in mole fractions of gas A in the two halves can be obtained by solving the differential equation defined by Fick's second law of diffusion. The result is

$$\overline{x}_U - \overline{x}_L = \frac{8}{\pi^2} \sum_{n=1}^{\infty} \frac{1}{(2n-1)^2} \exp -\left[\frac{(2n-1)^2 \pi^2 Dt}{4L^2}\right], \quad (1.D-1)$$

where $\overline{x}_U$ = average mole fraction of gas A in the upper section,

$\overline{x}_L$ = average mole fraction of gas A in the lower section,

D = diffusivity (m^2/s),

L = length of one-half cylinder (m),

t = time of diffusion (s),

π = 3.1416.

In an experiment the diffusivity of carbon dioxide in nitrous oxide was measured by the Löschmidt method. The diffusion cell had the dimension L = .1016 m. Initially the upper section was filled with carbon dioxide and the lower section with nitrous oxide. A sample of the experimental data is given below.

Average mole fraction of CO_2 in upper section .792

Average mole fraction of CO_2 in lower section .208

Time for diffusion 120 s

Temperature of system 25°C

Pressure of system 1 atm

Write a computer program to evaluate the diffusivity for CO_2-N_2O under the experimental conditions. Solve Eq. (1.D-1) by Newton's method.

(Suggestions: Eq. (1.D-1) involves the sum of an infinite series which converges rapidly. For computer calculations you may use the first five terms. Thus

$$f(D) \approx \overline{x}_U - \overline{x}_L - \frac{8}{\pi^2} \sum_{n=1}^{5} \frac{1}{(2n-1)^2} \exp\left[- \frac{(2n-1)^2 \pi^2 \, Dt}{4L^2}\right], \quad (1.D-2)$$

and the first derivative is

$$f'(D) \approx \frac{2t}{L^2} \sum_{n=1}^{5} \exp\left[- \frac{(2n-1)^2 \pi^2 \, Dt}{4L^2}\right]. \qquad (1.D-3)$$

Newton's method requires an initial guess of the value of D. Since the order of magnitude of the diffusivity of gases is 1×10^{-5} m^2/s, it is advisable to use D = 1.E-5 as the initial input.)

Answer: 1.17×10^{-5} m^2/s

1-E. In the bubble-point calculation of Example 1.3-2, we used an initially guessed temperature of $250^{\circ}F$. Both Newton's method and Muller's method (Example 1.5-1) converged to the desired solution, T = $262.99^{\circ}F$. Check to see what happens if we choose a starting value of T = $100^{\circ}F$. First use Newton's method, then Muller's method.

Answer: Newton's method may diverge with a bad initial guess. (See Figs. 1-12(a) and 1-12(b).) In this case it gives the value T = $888.26^{\circ}F$, which is an unreasonably high temperature.

64

Obviously this is not the solution that we
are looking for. Muller's method uses
successive parabolic approximations and
converges to the desired solution,
T = 262.99°F.

Chapter 2

Simultaneous Linear Equations

2.1 Introduction

In many engineering applications you will find it necessary
to solve a set of linear equations

$$\left.\begin{aligned}
a_{11}x_1 + a_{12}x_2 + \cdots + a_{1n}x_n &= b_1 \\
a_{21}x_1 + a_{22}x_2 + \cdots + a_{2n}x_n &= b_2 \\
\cdots\cdots\cdots\cdots\cdots\cdots\cdots\cdots\cdots \\
a_{n1}x_1 + a_{n2}x_2 + \cdots + a_{nn}x_n &= b_n
\end{aligned}\right\} \qquad (2.1\text{-}1)$$

We will assume the set of equations is prepared so that it has
a unique solution. We will discuss the Gauss-Jordan method
because it is easy to program. It is recommended that partial
pivoting (explained in the next section) be incorporated to
reduce truncation and round-off errors*.

The use of matrix notation is helpful. Recall that an
augmented matrix is formed by combining the n x n square matrix
containing the coefficients with the column matrix containing
the constants.

$$\text{Aug} = \begin{bmatrix}
a_{11} & a_{12} & \cdots & a_{1n} & b_1 \\
a_{21} & a_{22} & \cdots & a_{2n} & b_2 \\
\multicolumn{5}{c}{\cdots\cdots\cdots\cdots\cdots\cdots} \\
a_{n1} & a_{n2} & \cdots & a_{nn} & b_n
\end{bmatrix} \qquad (2.1\text{-}2)$$

---

*See Appendix at the end of the book.

In computer programming it is convenient to express the column

of b's simply as an additional column of a_{ij}'s. Thus

$$A = \begin{bmatrix} a_{11} & a_{12} & \cdots & a_{1n} & a_{1,n+1} \\ a_{21} & a_{22} & \cdots & a_{2n} & a_{2,n+1} \\ \cdots\cdots\cdots\cdots\cdots\cdots\cdots\cdots \\ a_{n1} & a_{n2} & \cdots & a_{nn} & a_{n,n+1} \end{bmatrix} \qquad (2.1-3)$$

2.2 Gauss-Jordan Elimination with Partial Pivoting

The method involves repeated use of the following three

steps.

Step 1. Partial pivoting

Let i = row index, j = column index, and k = pivot

index (k = 1, 2, ..., n). The main diagonal elements

are the pivot elements. The row in which the pivot element

lies is the pivot row, and the column in which the pivot

element lies is the pivot column. Starting from k = 1,

we scan the pivot column downward from the pivot element

a_{kk} to find the largest element a_{lk} ($k \leqslant l \leqslant n$) in absolute

value. If $l \neq k$, row k must be interchanged with row l.

This is equivalent to reordering the equations.

Step 2. Normalizing

The pivot row is divided by the pivot element. This

makes the diagonal element a_{kk} = 1.

Step 3. Eliminating

All elements in the pivot column are reduced to zero,

except the pivot element. This is accomplished by multi-plying the pivot equation by a factor a_{ik} ($i \neq k$). The resulting equations are subtracted, respectively, from the i-th equation. The process can be expressed by two equations:

$$factor = a_{ik}, \qquad\qquad\qquad (2.2\text{-}1)$$

$$a_{ij} \leftarrow a_{ij} - factor \cdot a_{kj}$$
$$(i \neq k, \; j = 1, 2, \ldots, n+1). \qquad (2.2\text{-}2)$$

Step 1 is repeated for the first (n - 1) columns. It is not necessary to scan column n. Steps 2 and 3 are repeated for k = 1, 2, ..., n. When elimination is complete, all diagonal elements have the value of 1. All other elements are zero, except the elements in the last column, which contains the solution values.

$$\begin{bmatrix} 1 & 0 & 0 & \cdots & 0 & a'_{1,n+1} \\ 0 & 1 & 0 & \cdots & 0 & a'_{2,n+1} \\ 0 & 0 & 1 & \cdots & 0 & a'_{3,n+1} \\ \cdots\cdots\cdots\cdots\cdots\cdots\cdots \\ 0 & 0 & 0 & \cdots & 1 & a'_{n,n+1} \end{bmatrix} \qquad (2.2\text{-}3)$$

We have

$$x_i = a'_{i,n+1} \; (i = 1, 2, \ldots, n). \qquad (2.2\text{-}4)$$

The above method is best illustrated by solving an example.

ILLUSTRATIVE EXAMPLE. Solve the following set of simultaneous linear equations by Gauss-Jordan elimination with partial pivoting.

$$2x_1 - 8x_2 + 3x_3 = -5$$
$$2x_1 - x_2 + 2x_3 = 6$$
$$x_1 + 6x_2 - x_3 = 10$$

First, we set up the augmented matrix as follows:

$$A = \begin{bmatrix} 2 & -8 & 3 & -5 \\ 2 & -1 & 2 & 6 \\ 1 & 6 & -1 & 10 \end{bmatrix}$$

The columns are considered in consecutive order for the purpose of partial pivotal condensation.

k = 1

Pivoting - Scanning column 1 we find that the largest element in absolute value is the diagonal element, $|a_{11}| = 2$. No row interchange is necessary.

Normalizing - We divide row 1 by a_{11}. The new matrix is

$$A = \begin{bmatrix} 1 & -4 & 1.5 & -2.5 \\ 2 & -1 & 2 & 6 \\ 1 & 6 & -1 & 10 \end{bmatrix}$$

Eliminating - All elements in column 1 are reduced to zero, except the pivot element, by using Eqs. (2.2-1) and (2.2-2).

i = 1   Since i = k, we skip row 1.

i = 2   Factor = a_{21} = 2. We multiply the pivot row, row 1, by 2. We then subtract the result from row 2 to produce zero in position (a_{21}).

i = 3   Factor = a_{31} = 1. We multiply row 1 by 1 and subtract the result from row 3 to produce zero in position (a_{31}).

The above operations give us a new matrix equivalent to the original matrix,

$$\begin{bmatrix} 1 & -4 & 1.5 & -2.5 \\ 0 & 7 & -1 & 11 \\ 0 & 10 & -2.5 & 12.5 \end{bmatrix}$$

k = 2

Pivoting - We scan column 2 downward from a_{22} to find the largest element in absolute value which is not on the main diagonal, $|a_{32}|$ = 10. We interchange row 2 with row 3.

$$\begin{bmatrix} 1 & -4 & 1.5 & -2.5 \\ 0 & 10 & -2.5 & 12.5 \\ 0 & 7 & -1 & 11 \end{bmatrix}$$

Note that elements already made zero are not affected.
Normalizing - We divide row 2 by a_{22}, the value of which is 10.

$$\begin{bmatrix} 1 & -4 & 1.5 & -2.5 \\ 0 & 1 & -0.25 & 1.25 \\ 0 & 7 & -1 & 11 \end{bmatrix}$$

Eliminating - We use Eqs. (2.2-1) and (2.2-2) to produce zeros in position (a_{12}) and (a_{32}). The new matrix is

$$\begin{bmatrix} 1 & 0 & 0.5 & 2.5 \\ 0 & 1 & -0.25 & 1.25 \\ 0 & 0 & 0.75 & 2.25 \end{bmatrix}$$

<u>k = 3</u>

Pivoting - Column 3 has no element below a_{33}. No scanning is necessary.

Normalizing - We divide row 3 by a_{33}, the value of which is 0.75.

$$\begin{bmatrix} 1 & 0 & 0.5 & 2.5 \\ 0 & 1 & -0.25 & 1.25 \\ 0 & 0 & 1 & 3 \end{bmatrix}$$

Eliminating - We use Eqs. (2.2-1) and (2.2-2) to produce zeros in positions (a_{13}) and (a_{23}).

$$\begin{bmatrix} 1 & 0 & 0 & 1 \\ 0 & 1 & 0 & 2 \\ 0 & 0 & 1 & 3 \end{bmatrix}$$

The last column of the final matrix is the solution vector:

$$x_1 = 1, \quad x_2 = 2, \quad x_3 = 3.$$

2.3 Flow Chart of Gauss-Jordan Elimination

A flow chart of Gauss-Jordan elimination with partial pivoting is shown in Figure 2-1. It is desirable to rearrange rows as required (partial pivoting) at each stage of the elimination process to reduce roundoff errors. The roundoff error may be further reduced with complete pivoting. This would involve interchange of columns as well as rows, thus causing additional complications in programming. Another possibility is to use double-precision arithmetic. The penalties are reduced computational speed and additional memory spaces. For solving a general set of equations, the compact method presented here is adequate.

2.4 Subroutine Gauss

SUBROUTINE GAUSS(A,X,N,NP1,M) is a subprogram for solving a system of n simultaneous, linear, algebraic equations in n unknowns by Gauss-Jordan elimination method with partial pivoting. It follows the flow chart of Figure 2-1 closely. The variable names used in the program are as follows:

A   Two-dimensional array containing elements of the augmented and reduced matrices,

C   Temporary name used for storing the value of an element before interchange is made,

I   Row index,

J   Column index,

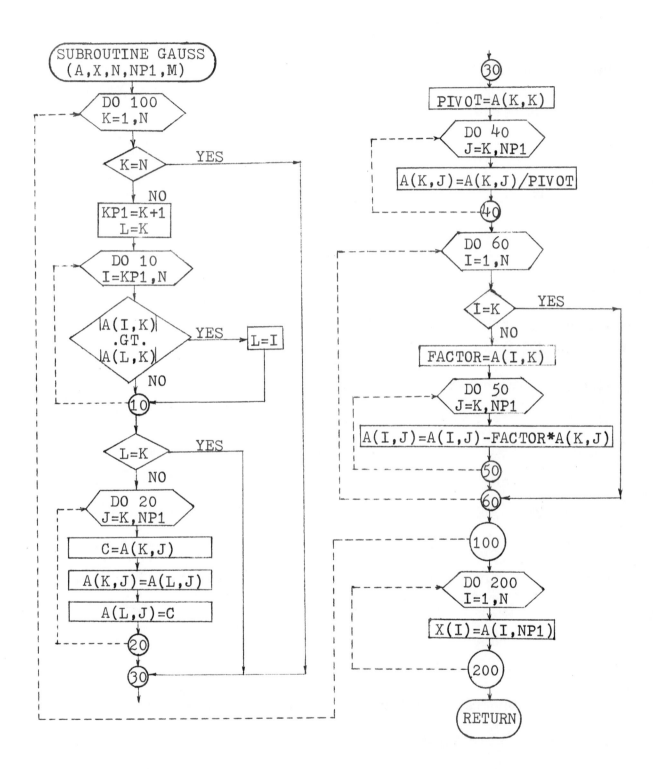

Figure 2-1.   Flow chart of Gauss-Jordan elimination
with partial pivoting

K   Pivot index,

L   Number of the row having the largest element (a_{1k}) in absolute value,

M   Row dimension of array A as it appears in the DIMENSION statement of the calling program,

N   Number of equations in the set being solved,

NP1   N + 1,

X   One-dimensional array containing the solution values.

Correct Dimensioning in Subprograms

The arguments of a subprogram may contain array names.   In the case of one-dimensional arrays, we dimension a variable in the subprogram as having one element even though it may have 100 elements in the calling program.   When we pass a two-dimensional array to a subroutine, the first dimension of the array must be the same in the DIMENSION statements of the two programs, whereas the second dimension need not be the same.   However, some systems require that corresponding array sizes be matched in both the calling program and the subprogram. The safest rule to follow is to use adjustable dimensions in the subprogram.   The variable specifying the size of the array in the subprogram appears as an additional argument.   This gives an automatic match of the dimensions of the dummy array with the dimensions of the actual array.

Table 2-1.   SUBROUTINE GAUSS

```
00100       SUBROUTINE GAUSS(A,X,N,NP1,M)
00110       DIMENSION A(M,1),X(1)
00120C
00130C      THIS SUBROUTINE SOLVES A SYSTEM OF N LINEAR
00140C      ALGEBRAIC EQUATIONS BY GAUSS-JORDAN ELIMINATION
00150C      WITH PARTIAL PIVOTING.
00160C      NP1=N+1.  A IS THE AUGMENTED MATRIX.  X IS THE
00170C      SOLUTION VECTOR.
00180C      M IS THE EXECUTION-TIME DIMENSION OF THE DUMMY ARRAY.
00190C
00200C      I=ROW INDEX, J=COLUMN INDEX, K=PIVOT INDEX.
00210C
00220C      PARTIAL PIVOTING --
00230C      SEARCH COLUMN K FROM A(K,K) DOWNWARD FOR THE
00240C      LARGEST ELEMENT, A(L,K), IN ABSOLUTE VALUE.
00250C      L IS THE ROW NUMBER WHICH CONTAINS THE LARGEST
00260C      ELEMENT.
00270C
00280       DO 100 K=1,N
00290C
00300C      ONLY (N-1) COLUMNS NEED TO BE SEARCHED.
00310C
00320       IF(K.EQ.N) GO TO 30
00330       KP1=K+1
00340       L=K
00350       DO 10 I=KP1,N
00360       IF(ABS(A(I,K)).GT.ABS(A(L,K))) L=I
00370    10 CONTINUE
00380C
00390C      CHECK TO SEE IF ROW INTERCGANGE IS NECESSARY.
00400C
00410       IF(L.EQ.K) GO TO 30
00420C
00430C      INTERCHANGE ROW K WITH ROW L.
00440C      ELEMENTS WHICH HAVE BEEN MADE ZERO ARE NOT
00450C      EFFECTED.  ONLY ELEMENTS FROM THE K-TH COLUMN
00460C      TO THE RIGHT NEED TO BE INTERCHANGED.
00465C
00470       DO 20 J=K,NP1
00480       C=A(K,J)
00490       A(K,J)=A(L,J)
00500       A(L,J)=C
00510    20 CONTINUE
00520C
00530C      NORMALIZING -- THE PIVOT ROW IS DIVIDED BY A(K,K).
00540C      ELEMENTS ALREADY MADE ZERO ARE NOT EFFECTED.
00550C      ALL DIAGONAL ELEMENTS ARE MADE 1.0.
00560C
00570    30 PIVOT=A(K,K)
00580       DO 40 J=K,NP1
00590       A(K,J)=A(K,J)/PIVOT
00600    40 CONTINUE
```

```
00681C
00682C        ELIMINATING -- ALL ELEMENTS IN THE PIVOT COLUMN
00683C        ARE MADE ZERO, EXCEPT THE PIVOT ELEMENT.
00684C
00685         DO 60 I=1,N
00686C
00687C        SKIP THE PIVOT ROW.
00688C
00690         IF(I.EQ.K) GO TO 60
00700         FACTOR=A(I,K)
00710C
00720C        ELEMENTS WHICH HAVE BEEN MADE ZERO PREVIOUSLY ARE
00730C        NOT EFFECTED.  ONLY ELEMENTS FROM THE K-TH COLUMN
00740C        TO THE RIGHT NEED TO BE CONSIDERED.
00750C
00760         DO 50 J=K,NP1
00770         A(I,J)=A(I,J)-FACTOR*A(K,J)
00780      50 CONTINUE
00790      60 CONTINUE
00800     100 CONTINUE
00810C
00820C        ELIMINATION IS COMPLETED.  THE LAST COLUMN OF THE
00830C        A-MATRIX CONTAINS THE N SOLUTION VALUES.
00840C
00850         DO 200 I=1,N
00860         X(I)=A(I,NP1)
00870     200 CONTINUE
00880         RETURN
00890         END
```

2.5 Program Solve

A FORTRAN IV program was written to solve a system of simultaneous equations. The listing is given in Table 2-2. PROGRAM SOLVE reads in the coefficients and the constants of an augmented matrix A. The main program calls in a subprogram, SUBROUTINE GAUSS, which solves the system of equations by the Gauss-Jordan elimination method.

PROGRAM SOLVE

Description of Input/Output

N   -(input) the number of equations

A   -(input) one-dimensional array containing elements of
           the augmented matrix

X   -(output) one-dimensional array containing the solution
           values

EXAMPLE 2.5-1. Simultaneous Linear Equations

Material and energy balances in a chemical process can be determined by solving the following set of simultaneous linear equations.

$$x + y - z = 8000$$

$$0.9x + 0.05y = 2680$$

$$1498x + 170y - 1198z = -130000$$

Evaluate x, y, and z by using PROGRAM SOLVE.

Table 2-2.   PROGRAM SOLVE

```
00100       PROGRAM SOLVE(INPUT,OUTPUT)
00110       DIMENSION A(10,11),X(10)
00120C
00130C      DATA INPUT
00140C
00150       READ*,N
00160       NP1=N+1
00170       READ*,((A(I,J),J=1,NP1),I=1,N)
00180C
00190C      CALL SUBROUTINE TO SOLVE THE PROBLEM.
00200C
00210       CALL GAUSS(A,X,N,NP1,10)
00220       PRINT 101,N,(X(I),I=1,N)
00230   101 FORMAT(//1X,"THE VALUES OF X(1) THROUGH X(",I2,
00240+      ") ARE"/(10X,F10.2))
00250       STOP
00260       END
00270C
00280C
00290C
00300C
00320       SUBROUTINE GAUSS(A,X,N,NP1,M)
00330       DIMENSION A(M,1),X(1)
00340       DO 100 K=1,N
00350       IF(K.EQ.N) GO TO 30
00360       KP1=K+1
00370       L=K
00380       DO 10 I=KP1,N
00390       IF(ABS(A(I,K)).GT.ABS(A(L,K))) L=I
00400    10 CONTINUE
00410       IF(L.EQ.K) GO TO 30
00420       DO 20 J=K,NP1
00430       C=A(K,J)
00440       A(K,J)=A(L,J)
00450       A(L,J)=C
00460    20 CONTINUE
00470    30 PIVOT=A(K,K)
00480       DO 40 J=K,NP1
00490       A(K,J)=A(K,J)/PIVOT
00500    40 CONTINUE
00510       DO 60 I=1,N
00520       IF(I.EQ.K) GO TO 60
00530       FACTOR=A(I,K)
00540       DO 50 J=K,NP1
00550       A(I,J)=A(I,J)-FACTOR*A(K,J)
00560    50 CONTINUE
00570    60 CONTINUE
00580   100 CONTINUE
00590       DO 200 I=1,N
00600       X(I)=A(I,NP1)
00610   200 CONTINUE
00620       RETURN
00630       END
```

78

Table 2-3. An application of PROGRAM SOLVE

DATA INPUT AT TIME OF EXECUTION

```
? 3
? 1., 1., -1., 8000.
? .9, .05, 0., 2680.
? 1498., 170., -1198., -130000.
```

OUTPUT

```
 THE VALUES OF X(1) THROUGH X( 3) ARE
            2413.68
           10153.80
            4567.48
```

The program was run with the following assignments given
to the variables:

   (1) N =3,

   (2) the coefficients and the constant terms to the
       subscripted variable A,

   (3) X_1 = x, X_2 = y, X_3 = z, elements of the subscripted
       variable X.

The solution vector was

$$x = 2413.68,$$

$$y = 10153.80,$$

$$z = 4567.48.$$

The computer printout is given in Table 2-3.

2.6 LU Decomposition

   The method of representing a set of equations in matrix
notation

$$AX = B \qquad\qquad (2.6-1)$$

and of solving by Gaussian elimination, or a variation of which,
is the standard procedure for the solution of simultaneous
linear equations. There is another method based on triangular
decomposition, in which the square matrix A is factored into
a lower triangular matrix L and an upper triangular matrix U,

$$A = LU. \qquad\qquad (2.6-2)$$

Substituting (2.6-2) into (2.6-1), we have

$$LUX = B. \qquad\qquad (2.6\text{-}3)$$

Once the L and U matrices have been found, Eq. (2.6-1) is solved in two stages. First we find a vector Y such that LY = B, and then we solve the set of equations UX = Y. Each of these involves the solution of a set of equations with a triangular matrix. The method is simple forward substitution or back substitution.

There is freedom in the choice of the diagonal values of L and U in Eq. (2.6-2). One popular method is to have all diagonal elements of the L-matrix equal to unity. The rest of the elements in both triangular matrices can then be uniquely determined.

$$
\begin{bmatrix}
a_{11} & a_{12} & \cdots & a_{1n} \\
a_{21} & a_{22} & \cdots & a_{2n} \\
\multicolumn{4}{c}{\cdots\cdots\cdots\cdots} \\
a_{n1} & a_{n2} & \cdots & a_{nn}
\end{bmatrix}
=
\begin{bmatrix}
1 & 0 & \cdots & 0 \\
\ell_{21} & 1 & \cdots & 0 \\
\multicolumn{4}{c}{\cdots\cdots\cdots\cdots} \\
\ell_{n1} & \ell_{n2} & \cdots & 1
\end{bmatrix}
\begin{bmatrix}
u_{11} & u_{12} & \cdots & u_{1n} \\
0 & u_{22} & \cdots & u_{2n} \\
\multicolumn{4}{c}{\cdots\cdots\cdots\cdots} \\
0 & 0 & \cdots & u_{nn}
\end{bmatrix}
\quad (2.6\text{-}4)
$$

The elements ℓ_{ik} and u_{ik} in Eq. (2.6-4) may be evaluated by matrix multiplication, followed by equating corresponding elements on both sides to obtain

$$
\left.
\begin{aligned}
u_{1k} &= a_{1k}, \quad 1 \leqslant k \leqslant n, \\[2mm]
\ell_{ik} &= \left(a_{ik} - \sum_{j=1}^{k-1} \ell_{ij} u_{jk}\right)\Big/ u_{kk}, \quad 2 \leqslant i \leqslant n, \quad 1 \leqslant k \leqslant i-1, \\[2mm]
u_{ik} &= a_{ik} - \sum_{j=1}^{i-1} \ell_{ij} u_{jk}, \quad 2 \leqslant i \leqslant n, \quad i \leqslant k \leqslant n.
\end{aligned}
\right\} \quad (2.6\text{-}5)
$$

Another possibility, of course, is to set the diagonal elements of the U-matrix equal to one. A third method is to set the diagonal elements of the L-matrix equal to the corresponding elements of the U-matrix.

The LU decomposition method will be illustrated by the example of Section 2.2, $AX = B$.

$$\begin{bmatrix} 2 & -8 & 3 \\ 2 & -1 & 2 \\ 1 & 6 & -1 \end{bmatrix} \begin{bmatrix} x_1 \\ x_2 \\ x_3 \end{bmatrix} = \begin{bmatrix} -5 \\ 6 \\ 10 \end{bmatrix} \qquad (2.6\text{-}6)$$

The coefficient matrix A is factored into L and U matrices with the diagonal elements of the L-matrix equal to unity. The nontrivial elements are obtained by means of Eq. (2.6-5).

$$u_{11} = a_{11} = 2,$$
$$u_{12} = a_{12} = -8,$$
$$u_{13} = a_{13} = 3,$$
$$\ell_{21} = a_{21}/u_{11} = 2/2 = 1,$$
$$u_{22} = a_{22} - \ell_{21}u_{12} = -1 - (1)(-8) = 7,$$
$$u_{23} = a_{23} - \ell_{21}u_{13} = 2 - (1)(3) = -1,$$
$$\ell_{31} = a_{31}/u_{11} = 1/2,$$
$$\ell_{32} = (a_{32} - \ell_{31}u_{12})/u_{22} = 10/7,$$
$$u_{33} = a_{33} - (\ell_{31}u_{13} + \ell_{32}u_{23}) = -15/14.$$

Thus $\quad L = \begin{bmatrix} 1 & 0 & 0 \\ 1 & 1 & 0 \\ \frac{1}{2} & \frac{10}{7} & 1 \end{bmatrix}$ and $\quad U = \begin{bmatrix} 2 & -8 & 3 \\ 0 & 7 & -1 \\ 0 & 0 & -\frac{15}{14} \end{bmatrix}.$

First we find the vector Y such that LY = B,

$$\begin{bmatrix} 1 & 0 & 0 \\ 1 & 1 & 0 \\ \frac{1}{2} & \frac{10}{7} & 1 \end{bmatrix} \begin{bmatrix} y_1 \\ y_2 \\ y_3 \end{bmatrix} = \begin{bmatrix} -5 \\ 6 \\ 10 \end{bmatrix}.$$

The results are

$$y_1 = b_1/l_{11} = -5/1 = -5,$$
$$y_2 = (b_2 - l_{21}y_1)/l_{22} = \left[6-(1)(-5)\right]/1 = 11,$$
$$y_3 = \left[b_3 - (l_{31}y_1 + l_{32}y_2)\right]/l_{33} = \left\{10 - \left[\frac{1}{2}(-5) + \frac{10}{7}(11)\right]\right\}/1 = -\frac{45}{14}.$$

Then we solve the set of equations UX = Y,

$$\begin{bmatrix} 2 & -8 & 3 \\ 0 & 7 & -1 \\ 0 & 0 & -\frac{15}{14} \end{bmatrix} \begin{bmatrix} x_1 \\ x_2 \\ x_3 \end{bmatrix} = \begin{bmatrix} -5 \\ 11 \\ -\frac{45}{14} \end{bmatrix},$$

whence

$$x_3 = \frac{y_3}{u_{33}} = \frac{-45/14}{-15/14} = 3,$$

$$x_2 = \frac{y_2 - u_{23}x_3}{u_{22}} = \frac{11-(-1)(3)}{7} = 2,$$

$$x_1 = \frac{y_1 - (u_{12}x_2 + u_{13}x_3)}{u_{11}} = \frac{-5 - \left[(-8)(2)+(3)(3)\right]}{2} = 1.$$

Gaussian elimination and triangular decomposition are direct methods based on elimination techniques. These methods are most suitable for small sets of equations with dense coefficient matrices. For the solution of a general set of equations, the number of operations for triangular decomposition is the same as that for Gaussian elimination. However, if the matrix is symmetric or sparse, the triangular decomposition method requires fewer arithmetic operations and less storage space. If a matrix has a special structure, more efficient algorithms can often be designed. An example is the Thomas algorithm for a tridiagonal matrix, which will be discussed in Section 2.7. For a large, randomly sparse matrix with no special structure, an iterative method, such as the Gauss-Seidel method, would probably be used.

For readers who want more details, the books by McCracken and Dorn (1964), and Conte and de Boor (1980) are recommended. A more extensive mathematical treatment is provided by the books of Issacson and Keller (1966), Ralston and Rabinowitz (1978), Ostrowski (1966), Forsythe and Moler (1967), and Ralston and Wilf (1960, 1967).

2.7 Tridiagonal Matrix

In many chemical engineering applications, such as the material and energy balances in distillation (Wang and Henke, 1966), gas absorption, or stirred tank reactors (Amundson, 1966), or the solution of simultaneous partial differential equations, a system of sparse set of equations may result.

$$\begin{aligned}
B_1 x_1 + C_1 x_2 &= D_1 \\
A_2 x_1 + B_2 x_2 + C_2 x_3 &= D_2 \\
A_3 x_2 + B_3 x_3 + C_3 x_4 &= D_3 \\
\cdots \cdots \cdots &\cdots \\
A_{n-1} x_{n-2} + B_{n-1} x_{n-1} + C_{n-1} x_n &= D_{n-1} \\
A_n x_{n-1} + B_n x_n &= D_n
\end{aligned} \right\} \quad (2.7\text{-}1)$$

Or in matrix notation as

$$\begin{bmatrix}
B_1 & C_1 & & & & \\
A_2 & B_2 & C_2 & & & \\
 & A_3 & B_3 & C_3 & & \\
 & & \cdots \cdots \cdots & & & \\
 & & & A_{n-1} & B_{n-1} & C_{n-1} \\
 & & & & A_n & B_n
\end{bmatrix}
\begin{bmatrix}
x_1 \\ x_2 \\ x_3 \\ \cdots \\ x_{n-1} \\ x_n
\end{bmatrix}
=
\begin{bmatrix}
D_1 \\ D_2 \\ D_3 \\ \cdots \\ D_{n-1} \\ D_n
\end{bmatrix}
\qquad (2.7\text{-}2)$$

The coefficient matrix which has nonzero elements on its
principal diagonal, superdiagonal, and subdiagonal, with zero
elements elsewhere, is called a tridiagonal matrix. A set of
linear equations represented by a tridiagonal matrix can be
solved by the highly efficient Thomas method, which uses the
following recurrence formulas.

$$p_1 = \frac{C_1}{B_1}, \qquad q_1 = \frac{D_1}{B_1}, \qquad\qquad (2.7\text{-}3)$$

$$p_j = \frac{C_j}{B_j - A_j p_{j-1}}, \quad 2 \leqslant j \leqslant n-1, \qquad (2.7\text{-}4)$$

$$q_j = \frac{D_j - A_j q_{j-1}}{B_j - A_j p_{j-1}}, \quad 2 \leqslant j \leqslant n. \tag{2.7-5}$$

After the p's and q's have been computed, the values of the x's are computed backward $(x_n, x_{n-1}, \ldots, x_2, x_1)$ as follows:

$$x_n = q_n, \tag{2.7-6}$$

$$x_k = q_k - p_k x_{k+1}, \quad (k = n-1, n-2, \ldots, 2, 1). \tag{2.7-7}$$

The Thomas method is easy to program, and it saves memory space by using four one-dimensional matrices, A, B, C, and D, to store the coefficients and the constants, instead of one large n x n matrix, since all the zeros need not be entered.

EXAMPLE 2.7-1. The Tridiagonal Matrix

Solve the following sparse set of equations, the coefficients of which can be represented by a tridiagonal matrix, by the Thomas method.

$$
\begin{array}{rcrcrcrcrcl}
4x_1 & + & x_2 & & & & & & & = & 1.2 \\
x_1 & - & 4x_2 & + & x_3 & & & & & = & -.31 \\
& & 3x_2 & + & 4x_3 & - & x_4 & & & = & 1.33 \\
& & & & - x_3 & - & x_4 & + & 4x_5 & = & .85 \\
& & & & & & 4x_4 & - & x_5 & = & .59
\end{array}
$$

We compare the above set of equations with Eq. (2.7-2). Nonzero coefficients appear only on the three diagonals. They are

A_2, A_3, A_4, A_5:   1, 3, -1, 4,

B_1, B_2, B_3, B_4, B_5: 4, -4, 4, -1, -1,

C_1, C_2, C_3, C_4:   1, 1, -1, 4.

The constant terms are

D_1, D_2, D_3, D_4, D_5: 1.2, -.31, 1.33, .85, .59.

PROGRAM TDMX was written to solve a set of linear equations represented by a tridiagonal matrix, by using the Thomas algorithm. The list of the program is given in Table 2-4.

PROGRAM TDMX

Description of Input/Output

N   -(input) the number of equations

A   -(input) one-dimensional array containing elements on
        the subdiagonal (The value of A_1, which is zero, must
        be entered.)

B   -(input) one-dimensional array containing elements on
        the principal diagonal

C   -(input) one-dimensional array containing elements on
        the superdiagonal (The value of C_n, which is zero,
        must be entered.)

D   -(input) one-dimensional array containing the constants

X   -(output) one-dimensional array containing elements of
        the solution vector

The program was run. It gave the following solution set:

Table 2-4.   PROGRAM TDMX

```
00100         PROGRAM TDMX(INPUT,OUTPUT)
00110         DIMENSION A(10),B(10),C(10),D(10),X(10)
00120C
00130C        DATA INPUT
00140C
00150         READ*,N
00160         READ*,(A(I),I=1,N)
00170         READ*,(B(I),I=1,N)
00180         READ*,(C(I),I=1,N)
00190         READ*,(D(I),I=1,N)
00200C
00210C        SOLVE SET OF EQUATIONS BY THOMAS METHOD.
00220C
00230         CALL THOMAS(N,A,B,C,D,X)
00240C
00250C        OUTPUT
00260C
00270         PRINT 10,(X(I),I=1,N)
00280      10 FORMAT(//5X,"THE VALUES OF X(1) THROUGH X(N) ARE"//
00290+        (5X,5F10.3))
00300         STOP
00310         END
00320C
00330C
00340C
00350C
00370         SUBROUTINE THOMAS(N,A,B,C,D,X)
00380         DIMENSION A(1),B(1),C(1),D(1),X(1),P(10),Q(10)
00390C
00400C        COMPUTE P(1) AND Q(1)
00410C
00420         P(1)=C(1)/B(1)
00430         Q(1)=D(1)/B(1)
00440C
00450C        COMPUTE P(2) THROUGH P(N-1) AND Q(2) THROUGH Q(N).
00460C
00470         N1=N-1
00480         DO 10 J=2,N1
00490         R=B(J)-A(J)*P(J-1)
00500         P(J)=C(J)/R
00510      10 Q(J)=(D(J)-A(J)*Q(J-1))/R
00520         Q(N)=(D(N)-A(N)*Q(N-1))/(B(N)-A(N)*P(N-1))
00530C
00540C        COMPUTE X(N).
00550C
00560         X(N)=Q(N)
00570C
00580C        COMPUTE X(N-1) THROUGH X(1).
00590C
00600         DO 20 J=1,N1
00610         K=N-J
00620      20 X(K)=Q(K)-P(K)*X(K+1)
00630         RETURN
00640         END
```

88

Table 2-5. An application of PROGRAM TDMX

DATA INPUT AT TIME OF EXECUTION

```
? 5
? 0., 1., 3., -1., 4.
? 4., -4., 4., -1., -1.
? 1., 1., -1., 4., 0.
? 1.2, -.31, 1.33, .85, .59
```

OUTPUT

THE VALUES OF X(1) THROUGH X(N) ARE

.250   .200   .240   .230   .330

$$x_1 = .25,$$

$$x_2 = .20,$$

$$x_3 = .24,$$

$$x_4 = .23,$$

$$x_5 = .33.$$

The computer printout is listed in Table 2-5.

2.8 Homogeneous Equations and Matrix Eigenvalue Problems

Mathematical analysis of chemical engineering problems (Amundson 1966) sometimes leads to a set of homogeneous linear equations of the form

$$
\left.
\begin{aligned}
a_{11}x_1 + a_{12}x_2 + \cdots + a_{1n}x_n &= \lambda x_1 \\
a_{21}x_1 + a_{22}x_2 + \cdots + a_{2n}x_n &= \lambda x_2 \\
\cdots\cdots\cdots\cdots\cdots\cdots\cdots\cdots\cdots\cdots\cdots \\
a_{n1}x_1 + a_{n2}x_2 + \cdots + a_{nn}x_n &= \lambda x_n
\end{aligned}
\right\} . \qquad (2.8\text{-}1)
$$

Written in matrix notation, Eq. (2.8-1) becomes

$$AX = \lambda X,$$

or

$$(A - \lambda I)X = 0. \qquad (2.8\text{-}2)$$

Since we are interested only in nontrivial solutions, it is necessary that the determinant of $(A - \lambda I)$ be equal to zero, i.e.,

$$
\begin{vmatrix}
a_{11}-\lambda & a_{12} & \cdots & a_{1n} \\
a_{21} & a_{22}-\lambda & \cdots & a_{2n} \\
\cdots\cdots\cdots\cdots\cdots\cdots\cdots\cdots\cdots \\
a_{n1} & a_{n2} & \cdots & a_{nn}-\lambda
\end{vmatrix} = 0. \qquad (2.8\text{-}3)
$$

The expansion of the determinant in (2.8-3) produces a polynomial in λ of degree n. This polynomial equation is known as
the characteristic equation of the matrix A. The eigenvalues λ
are the roots of this equation. The solution of Eq. (2.8-1)
then gives the eigenvector X.

With linear equations our interest is just to find the
solution. With eigenvalue problems there are many possibilities.
We may require only one particular eigenvalue, or only the
largest or smallest eigenvalue, or all of the eigenvalues and
their eigenvectors.

Unless n is small, the solution of eigenvalue problems by
finding the roots of the characteristic polynomial is usually
not a satisfactory approach. There are some highly effective
techniques based on transformations which reduce the matrix to
a simpler form. The transformed matrix can easily be solved
to find the eigenvalues. Numerical treatment of problems
involving symmetric matrices has been well developed. The most
efficient methods include Householder's method (1953) to reduce
the matrix to a tridiagonal form, the LR transformation
(Rutishauser 1958) which repeatedly decomposes a matrix into

the product of a lower triangular matrix and an upper triangular matrix, and the QR factorization (Francis 1961/1962) in which a matrix is decomposed into the product of an orthogonal matrix and an upper triangular matrix. Usually we select the most appropriate method for a particular problem.

It is beyond the scope of this book to discuss the large variety of methods available. The reader is referred to the book of Wilkinson (1965), which gives a full account of the methods. The book of Schwarz and others, translated by Hertelendy (1973), contains sixteen computer programs, originally written in the ALGOL language, converted into the FORTRAN IV language counterpart by the translator. These programs have been tested and are generally reliable. It is not recommended that the reader should attempt to write his own program.

PROBLEM

2-A. Consider the multicomponent distillation process that is
depicted schematically in Figure P2-A.

Let F = flow rate of the feed,

   K = vapor-liquid equilibrium ratio, y/x,

   L = flow rate of the liquid stream,

   n = number of equilibrium stages,

   noc = number of components,

   V = flow rate of the vapor stream,

   W_1 = flow rate of the overhead product,

   W_2 = flow rate of the bottoms product ($W_2 = L_{10}$),

   x = mole fraction of a component in the liquid phase,

   y = mole fraction of a component in the vapor phase,

   z = mole fraction of a component in the feed.

Subscripts

   i = the i-th component,

   j = the j-th stage.

We write the following material balances from stage to stage
for each component: (i = 1, 2, ..., noc)

$$\left. \begin{aligned}
-(L_1 + W_1)x_{i,1} + V_2 y_{i,2} &= 0, \\
L_{j-1}x_{i,j-1} - L_j x_{i,j} - V_j y_{i,j} + V_{j+1}y_{i,j+1} &= 0, \\
(2 \leqslant j \leqslant 5, \quad 7 \leqslant j \leqslant 9), & \\
L_5 x_{i,5} - L_6 x_{i,6} - V_6 y_{i,6} + V_7 y_{i,7} &= -F z_i, \\
L_9 x_{i,9} - L_{10}x_{i,10} - V_{10}y_{i,10} &= 0.
\end{aligned} \right\} \quad (2.A\text{-}1)$$

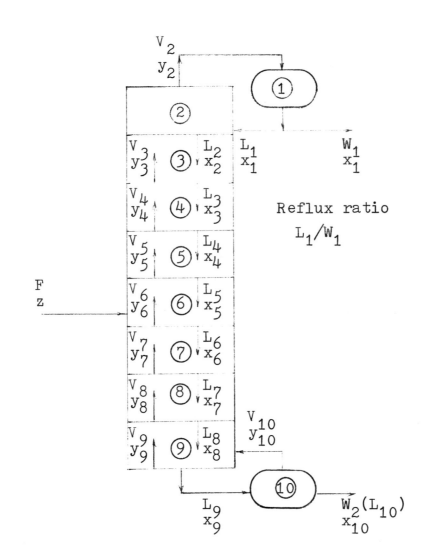

Figure P2-A. Multicomponent distillation

(Note: Variables x and y have two subscripts. The first
subscript refers to the i-th component; the second refers
to the j-th stage. Here the subscript i is omitted for
simplicity. Variables L and V have one subscript,
which refers to the j-th stage. Variable z has one
subscript, which refers to the i-th component. The
subscript i is omitted for simplicity.)

The equilibrium relations are

$$y_{i,j} = K_{i,j}x_{i,j}, \quad 1 \leqslant i \leqslant noc, \quad 1 \leqslant j \leqslant n. \qquad (2.A-2)$$

Eliminating y between Eqs. (2.A-1) and (2.A-2), we obtain

$$\left.\begin{aligned}
&-(L_1 + W_1)x_{i,1} + V_2 K_{i,2}x_{i,2} = 0, \\
&L_{j-1}x_{i,j-1} - (L_j + K_{i,j}V_j)x_{i,j} + K_{i,j+1}V_{j+1}x_{i,j+1} = 0, \\
&\qquad 2 \leqslant j \leqslant 5, \quad 7 \leqslant j \leqslant 9, \\
&L_5 x_{i,5} - (L_6 + K_{i,6}V_6)x_{i,6} + K_{i,7}V_7 x_{i,7} = -Fz_i, \\
&L_9 x_{i,9} - (L_{10} + K_{i,10}V_{10})x_{i,10} = 0.
\end{aligned}\right\} \quad (2.A-3)$$

Eq. (2.A-3) is a set of equations whose coefficient matrix is tridiagonal. Written in matrix notation, it becomes

$$\begin{bmatrix}
B_{i,1} & C_{i,1} & & & & & \\
A_{i,2} & B_{i,2} & C_{i,2} & & & & \\
& \cdots & \cdots & \cdots & & & \\
& & A_{i,j} & B_{i,j} & C_{i,j} & & \\
& & & \cdots & \cdots & \cdots & \\
& & & & A_{i,9} & B_{i,9} & C_{i,9} \\
& & & & & A_{i,10} & B_{i,10}
\end{bmatrix}
\begin{bmatrix}
x_{i,1} \\
x_{i,2} \\
\cdots \\
x_{i,j} \\
\cdots \\
x_{i,9} \\
x_{i,10}
\end{bmatrix}
=
\begin{bmatrix}
D_{i,1} \\
D_{i,2} \\
\cdots \\
D_{i,j} \\
\cdots \\
D_{i,9} \\
D_{i,10}
\end{bmatrix}, \quad (2.A-4)$$

where $A_{i,1} = 0$,

$$A_{i,j} = L_{j-1}, \quad 2 \leqslant j \leqslant 10,$$

$$B_{i,1} = -(L_1 + W_1),$$

$$B_{i,j} = -(L_j + K_{i,j}V_j), \quad 2 \leqslant j \leqslant 10,$$

$$C_{i,j} = K_{i,j+1} V_{j+1}, \quad 1 \leqslant j \leqslant 9,$$

$$C_{i,10} = 0,$$

$$D_{i,j} = 0, \quad 1 \leqslant j \leqslant 10, \quad j \neq 6,$$

$$D_{i,6} = -Fz_i.$$

Write a computer program to solve Eq. (2.A-4) by the Thomas algorithm. Notice that there are (noc) components. Eq. (2.A-4) is to be solved (noc) times, each time with different values of $A_{i,j}$, $B_{i,j}$, $C_{i,j}$, and $D_{i,j}$.

The following test data are provided for you to determine the validity of your program.

(a) The feed, overhead, and bottoms product rates are

$$F = 100, \quad W_1 = 50, \quad W_2 = 50.$$

(b) The feed consists of five components, whose mole fractions are $z_1 = .055$, $z_2 = .165$, $z_3 = .227$, $z_4 = .218$, $z_5 = .335$.

(c) The number of equilibrium stages is ten, including the total condenser and the partial reboiler. The total condenser is stage no. 1 and the reboiler is stage no. 10. The initial temperature guesses are ($^\circ$F)

$$T_1 = 132, \quad T_2 = 164, \quad T_3 = 172, \quad T_4 = 180, \quad T_5 = 188,$$

$$T_6 = 196, \quad T_7 = 204, \quad T_8 = 212, \quad T_9 = 220, \quad T_{10} = 228.$$

(d) The reflux ratio is 2.5. Assume constant molal overflow. The initially guessed liquid flow rates are

$$L_1 = L_2 = L_3 = L_4 = L_5 = 125,$$

$$L_6 = L_7 = L_8 = L_9 = 225, \quad L_{10} = W_2 = 50.$$

(e) The vapor flow rates are obtained by overall mass balances,

$V_1 = 0$, V_2 through $V_{10} = 175$.

(f) Equilibrium relations can be represented by

$$K_{i,j} = \alpha_i + \beta_i T_j + \gamma_i T_j^2.$$

The coefficients for each individual component are

Component i	α_i	β_i	γ_i
1	0.70	0.30×10^{-2}	0.60×10^{-4}
2	2.21	1.95×10^{-2}	0.90×10^{-4}
3	1.50	-1.60×10^{-2}	0.80×10^{-4}
4	0.86	-0.97×10^{-2}	0.46×10^{-4}
5	0.71	-0.87×10^{-2}	0.42×10^{-4}

Sample answers:

Stage no. 1

$x_{1,1} = .10990$

$x_{2,1} = .32144$

$x_{3,1} = .41204$

$x_{4,1} = .05670$

$x_{5,1} = .03407$

Sum $= .93415$

Stage no. 10

$x_{1,10} = .00009$

$x_{2,10} = .00856$

$x_{3,10} = .04196$

$x_{4,10} = .37930$

$x_{5,10} = .63593$

Sum $= 1.06584$

Note: The solution of the component mass balances by tridiagonal matrix is only one of the many steps involved in multicomponent distillation calculations. With a set of initially guessed values of T and L (The V's are obtained by overall mass balances.), Eq. (2.A-4) can readily be solved. However, the requirement that the summation of mole fractions on each stage be unity, $\sum x_{i,j} = 1$, is not satisfied. To achieve this requirement, a convergence method must be incorporated, such as the bubble-point subroutine to correct the T's or the energy balance subroutine to correct the L's and V's. For detailed treatments of this subject the reader is referred to Wang and Henke (1966), King (1980), and Holland (1975).

Chapter 3

Curve Fitting Using the Method of Least Squares

3.1 Linear Regression

Often it is necessary for us to find a functional relation $y = f(x)$ which best approximates a set of n data points (x_i, y_i). For the simplest case of one independent variable, a straight line

$$y = a + bx \qquad (3.1-1)$$

may be used. The difference between the data value, y_i, and that represented by the equation is

$$\delta_i = y_i - (a + bx_i) \qquad (3.1-2)$$

By the principle of least squares, the equation will best fit the data when the sum of the squares of the errors is a minimum.

$$s = \sum_{i=1}^{n} (\delta_i)^2 = \sum_{i=1}^{n} \left[y_i - (a + bx_i) \right]^2 \qquad (3.1-3)$$

One condition for s to be minimum is that the partial derivatives of s with respect to a and b must be zero. Thus

$$\frac{\partial s}{\partial a} = \sum_{i=1}^{n} 2 \left[y_i - (a + bx_i) \right] (-1) = 0.$$

$$\frac{\partial s}{\partial b} = \sum_{i=1}^{n} 2 \left[y_i - (a + bx_i) \right] (-x_i) = 0.$$

Simplifying, we get

$$n \cdot a + \left(\sum x_i \right) b = \sum y_i, \qquad (3.1-4)$$

99

$$(\sum x_i)a + (\sum x_i^2)b = \sum x_i y_i . \qquad (3.1-5)$$

Solving Eqs. (3.1-4) and (3.1-5) simultaneously, we obtain

$$b = \frac{n(\sum x_i y_i) - (\sum x_i)(\sum y_i)}{n(\sum x_i^2) - (\sum x_i)^2} , \qquad (3.1-6)$$

$$a = \frac{(\sum y_i) - b(\sum x_i)}{n} . \qquad (3.1-7)$$

Eqs. (3.1-4) and (3.1-5) are called normal equations. Their solutions, Eqs. (3.1-6) and (3.1-7), when substituted into Eq. (3.1-1), will produce the linear least squares curve fit. This is also called the linear regression function of y on x.

Equations that can be transformed to the linear form

Sometimes it is possible to transform a nonlinear equation to the linear form by proper substitutions. A few examples follow.

$y = ab^x$ Taking logarithms we get

$$\ln y = \ln a + x(\ln b).$$

Now let

$$z = \ln y,$$
$$A = \ln a,$$
$$B = \ln b.$$

So $z = A + Bx.$

This equation is linear in x and z.

$y = ax^b$ Taking logarithms we have

$$\ln y = \ln a + b(\ln x).$$

Let

$$z = \ln y,$$

$$A = \ln a,$$

$$t = \ln x.$$

Then $z = A + bt.$

Again, this equation is linear in t and z.

$y = \dfrac{1}{a + bx}$ If we let

$$z = \frac{1}{y},$$

then $z = a + bx.$

This equation is linear in x and z.

The least squares method may be applied to each of the above cases.

EXAMPLE 3.1-1.   Constant Pressure Heat Capacity of Ethylene Glycol as a Function of Temperature

The specific heat capacity of ethylene glycol as a function of temperature at 1 atm pressure is given in the following:

T, °C	C_p, cal/(g)(°C)
-40	0.507
0	0.551
50	0.611
100	0.667
150	0.725
200	0.780

Fit the empirical equation C_p = a + bT to the data using the method of least squares. Find the coefficients a and b.

FORTRAN IV PROGRAM CP (see Table 3-1) was written to fit the linear equation y = a + bx to n data points (x_i, y_i) by the method of least squares.

PROGRAM CP

Description of Input/Output

N   -(input) the number of data points

X   -(input) one-dimensional array containing the data
      values of the independent variable (temperature)

Y   -(input) one-dimensional array containing the data
      values of the dependent variable (heat capacity)

A,B -(output) coefficients of the fitted equation

YC   -(output) one-dimensional array containing the fitted
      values of the dependent variable (heat capacity from
      the equation)

The input data are to be entered in the following order:

        N,(X(I),Y(I),I=1,N)

Table 3-1. PROGRAM CP

```
00100        PROGRAM CP(INPUT,OUTPUT)
00110        DIMENSION X(10),Y(10),YC(10)
00120C
00130C       DATA INPUT
00140C
00150        READ*,N
00160        READ*,(X(I),Y(I),I=1,N)
00170C
00180C       METHOD OF LEAST SQUARES FIT
00190C
00200        SUMX=0.
00210        SUMY=0.
00220        SUMXY=0.
00230        SUMXX=0.
00240        DO 10 I=1,N
00250        SUMX=SUMX+X(I)
00260        SUMY=SUMY+Y(I)
00270        SUMXY=SUMXY+X(I)*Y(I)
00280     10 SUMXX=SUMXX+X(I)*X(I)
00290        B=(N*SUMXY-SUMX*SUMY)/(N*SUMXX-SUMX*SUMX)
00300        A=(SUMY-B*SUMX)/N
00310        DO 20 I=1,N
00320     20 YC(I)=A+B*X(I)
00330C
00340C       OUTPUT
00350C
00360        PRINT 30
00370     30 FORMAT(//5X,"THE FITTED EQUATION IS Y(I) = A + B*X(I)")
00380        PRINT 40,A,B
00390     40 FORMAT(/8X,"A =",E15.5,5X,"B =",E15.5)
00400        PRINT 50,(X(I),Y(I),YC(I),I=1,N)
00410     50 FORMAT(//10X,"X(I)",6X,"Y(I)",6X,"YC(I)"/
00420+        (5X,F10.1,2F10.3))
00430        STOP
00440        END
```

Table 3-2. An application of PROGRAM CP

DATA INPUT AT TIME OF EXECUTION

? 6
? -40., .507
? 0., .551
? 50., .611
? 100., .667
? 150., .725
? 200., .780

OUTPUT

THE FITTED EQUATION IS Y(I) = A + B*X(I)

A =   .55254E+00   B =   .11430E-02

X(I)	Y(I)	YC(I)
-40.0	.507	.507
0.0	.551	.553
50.0	.611	.610
100.0	.667	.667
150.0	.725	.724
200.0	.780	.781

PROGRAM CP was run to solve Example 3.1-1. The computer printout (see Table 3-2) gave

$$A = 0.55254,$$

$$B = 0.001143.$$

The data values and the fitted values of the heat capacity were printed out together to allow us to determine the goodness-of-fit.

Y(I)	YC(I)
.507	.507
.551	.553
.611	.610
.667	.667
.725	.724
.780	.781

It appears that the straight line relation offers a sufficiently close fit.

EXAMPLE 3.1-2. <u>Vapor Pressure of Benzene vs. Temperature</u>

The variation of vapor pressure vs. temperature can be expressed approximately by an empirical equation of the form

$$\log_{10} P = A + \frac{B}{T},$$

where P = vapor pressure,

T = absolute temperature,

A, B = empirical constants.

Write a computer program to obtain the best fit of the following
vapor pressure data of benzene vs. temperature. Determine the
constants A and B by the method of least squares.

Temp., $^{\circ}$C	v.p., mm Hg
7.6	40
15.4	60
26.1	100
42.2	200
60.6	400
80.1	760

First we linearize the correlation by the following
substitutions.

Let

$$X = \frac{1}{T(^{\circ}C) + 273.15},$$

$$Y = \log_{10} P.$$

The resulting equation is $Y = A + BX$, which is linear in X
and Y. The procedure used in the preceeding example can be
applied.

PROGRAM VP (see Table 3-3) was written and was run to
solve Example 3.1-2.

PROGRAM VP

Description of Input/Output

N   -(input) the number of data points

T   -(input) one-dimensional array containing the temp-
        erature (°C) (The computer program converts the
        temperature to °K.)

P   -(input) one-dimensional array containing the vapor
        pressure (mm Hg)

X   -(intermediate calculation) one-dimensional array
        containing the independent variable

Y   -(intermediate calculation) one-dimensional array
        containing the dependent variable

A,B   -(output) the fitted coefficients

PCAL   -(output) one-dimensional array containing the fitted
        vapor pressure (calculated from the equation)

The input data are to be entered in the following order:

    N,(T(I),P(I),I=1,N)

    The computer printout (see Table 3-4) gives

            A = 7.840778,

            B = -0.17493626 x 10^4.

It also computes the fitted vapor pressures PCAL(I) for a

comparison check.

P(I)	PCAL(I)
40.0	40.71
60.0	60.00
100.0	98.84
200.0	196.52
400.0	397.41
760.0	773.72

Table 3-3. PROGRAM VP

```
00100       PROGRAM VP(INPUT,OUTPUT)
00110       DIMENSION T(10),P(10),X(10),Y(10),PCAL(10)
00120C
00130C      DATA INPUT
00140C
00150       READ*,N
00160       READ*,(T(I),P(I),I=1,N)
00170C
00180C      METHOD OF LEAST SQUARES FIT
00190C
00200       SUMX=0.
00210       SUMY=0.
00220       SUMXY=0.
00230       SUMXX=0.
00240       DO 10 I=1,N
00250       X(I)=1./(T(I)+273.15)
00260       Y(I)=ALOG10(P(I))
00270       SUMX=SUMX+X(I)
00280       SUMY=SUMY+Y(I)
00290       SUMXY=SUMXY+X(I)*Y(I)
00300    10 SUMXX=SUMXX+X(I)*X(I)
00310       B=(N*SUMXY-SUMX*SUMY)/(N*SUMXX-SUMX*SUMX)
00320       A=(SUMY-B*SUMX)/N
00330       DO 20 I=1,N
00340    20 PCAL(I)=10.**(A+B*X(I))
00350C
00360C      OUTPUT
00370C
00380       PRINT 30
00390    30 FORMAT(//" THE FITTED EQUATION IS")
00400       PRINT 40,A,B
00410    40 FORMAT(//"      ALOG10(P(I)) = (",E16.8,
00420+      " ) + (",E16.8," )/(T(I)+273.15)")
00430       PRINT 50
00440    50 FORMAT(//"      T(I)",6X,"P(I)",3X,"PCAL(I)")
00450       PRINT 60,(T(I),P(I),PCAL(I),I=1,N)
00460    60 FORMAT(3F10.2)
00470       STOP
00480       END
```

Table 3-4. An application of PROGRAM VP

DATA INPUT AT TIME OF EXECUTION

? 6
? 7.6, 40.
? 15.4, 60.
? 26.1, 100.
? 42.2, 200.
? 60.6, 400.
? 80.1, 760.

OUTPUT

THE FITTED EQUATION IS

$$ALOG10(P(I)) = (\quad .78407780E+01\ ) + (\quad -.17493626E+04\ )/(T(I)+273.15)$$

T(I)	P(I)	PCAL(I)
7.60	40.00	40.71
15.40	60.00	60.00
26.10	100.00	98.84
42.20	200.00	196.52
60.60	400.00	397.41
80.10	760.00	773.72

It appears that the fit is fairly good. (A later example shows that an improved fit can be obtained by using the Antoine equation. See Example 3.3-2.)

3.2 Polynomial Regression

We wish to approximate n data points (x_i, y_i) by a polynomial of degree m $(m < n)$.

$$y(x) = c_1 + c_2 x + c_3 x^2 + \ldots + c_m x^{m-1} + c_{m+1} x^m \quad (3.2-1)$$

Applying the principle of least squares, we obtain the following normal equations:

$$
\left.
\begin{aligned}
n c_1 + (\textstyle\sum x_i) c_2 + \ldots + (\textstyle\sum x_i^m) c_{m+1} &= \textstyle\sum y_i \\
(\textstyle\sum x_i) c_1 + (\textstyle\sum x_i^2) c_2 + \ldots + (\textstyle\sum x_i^{m+1}) c_{m+1} &= \textstyle\sum x_i y_i \\
\cdots\cdots\cdots\cdots\cdots\cdots\cdots\cdots\cdots\cdots\cdots\cdots\cdots \\
(\textstyle\sum x_i^m) c_1 + (\textstyle\sum x_i^{m+1}) c_2 + \ldots + (\textstyle\sum x_i^{2m}) c_{m+1} &= \textstyle\sum x_i^m y_i
\end{aligned}
\right\} (3.2-2)
$$

There are (m+1) linear equations in (m+1) unknowns, c_1, c_2, ..., c_{m+1}. Eq. (3.2-2) may be solved by the Gauss-Jordan elimination method described in Section 2.2. The augmented matrix is

$$
A = \begin{bmatrix}
n & \sum x_i & \sum x_i^2 & \cdots & \sum x_i^m & \sum y_i \\
\sum x_i & \sum x_i^2 & \sum x_i^3 & \cdots & \sum x_i^{m+1} & \sum x_i y_i \\
\cdots & \cdots & \cdots & \cdots & \cdots & \cdots \\
\sum x_i^m & \sum x_i^{m+1} & \sum x_i^{m+2} & \cdots & \sum x_i^{2m} & \sum x_i^m y_i
\end{bmatrix} \quad (3.2-3)
$$

Examining Eq. (3.2-3), we find that all elements of the coefficient matrix are the sums of x_i's or x_i's raised to some power except the first element, a_{11}, which is n. The last column, the (m+2)th column, is the constant vector, which contains the sums of the products of x_i^l and y_i (l = 0, 1, 2, ..., m).

Let

$$\text{SUMX}(1) \qquad = \sum x_i$$

$$\text{SUMX}(2) \qquad = \sum x_i^2$$

$$\text{SUMX}(3) \qquad = \sum x_i^3$$

· · · · · · · · · · · · · · ·

$$\text{SUMX}(2m) \qquad = \sum x_i^{2m}$$

There are 2m SUMX's.

$$\text{SUMXY}(1) \quad = \sum x_i^0 y_i = \sum y_i$$

$$\text{SUMXY}(2) \quad = \sum x_i y_i$$

$$\text{SUMXY}(3) \quad = \sum x_i^2 y_i$$

· · · · · · · · · · · · · · · · · ·

$$\text{SUMXY}(m+1) = \sum x_i^m y_i$$

There are (m+1) SUMXY's.

In computer calculations these summations are conveniently handled with DO loops. For the SUMXY's we have one number that is raised to the zero power. If that number is zero itself, an error message will result. Therefore we choose to compute SUMXY(1) separately. After all the summations have

been completed, we will load them into the augmented matrix
in the right positions.

Let

$\qquad$ i = row index,

$\qquad$ j = column index,

and $\qquad$ k = i + j - 2.

Every element a_{ij} of the augmented matrix can be represented
by one of the following three equations.

$$a_{11} = n \qquad\qquad\qquad (3.2\text{-}4)$$

$$a_{ij} = SUMX(k)$$
$$\begin{cases} i = 1, 2, 3, \ldots, m+1 \\ j = 1, 2, 3, \ldots, m+1 \\ k = i + j - 2 > 0 \end{cases}$$
$$\qquad\qquad\qquad (3.2\text{-}5)$$

$$a_{i,m+2} = SUMXY(i)$$
$$i = 1, 2, 3, \ldots, m+1 \qquad\qquad (3.2\text{-}6)$$

A flow chart of SUBROUTINE MATRIX is given in Figure 3-1.
A listing of the program is given in Table 3-5. The subprogram
is used to generate the augmented matrix of the (m+1) normal
equations in the polynomial regression process.

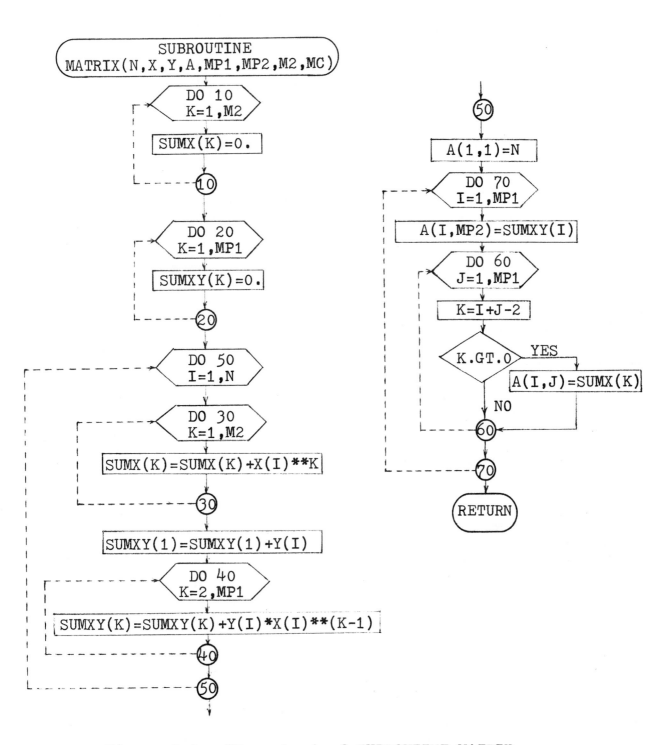

Figure 3-1.   Flow chart of SUBROUTINE MATRIX

113

Table 3-5. SUBROUTINE MATRIX

```
00100        SUBROUTINE MATRIX(N,X,Y,A,MP1,MP2,M2,MC)
00110C
00120C       THIS PROGRAM GENERATES THE AUGMENTED MATRIX OF
00130C       THE (M+1) NORMAL EQUATIONS FOR POLYNOMIAL REGRESSION
00140C       OF DEGREE M.
00150C
00160        DIMENSION X(1),Y(1),A(MC,1),SUMX(20),SUMXY(11)
00170C
00180C       CLEAR VARIABLES SUMX AND SUMXY.
00190C
00200        DO 10 K=1,M2
00210     10 SUMX(K)=0.
00220        DO 20 K=1,MP1
00230     20 SUMXY(K)=0.
00240C
00250C       COMPUTE SUMS.
00260C
00270        DO  50 I=1,N
00280        DO 30 K=1,M2
00290     30 SUMX(K)=SUMX(K)+X(I)**K
00300C
00310C       SUMXY(1) IS TREATED SEPARATELY.
00320C
00330        SUMXY(1)=SUMXY(1)+Y(I)
00340C
00350C       COMPUTE OTHER SUMXY'S.
00360C
00370        DO 40 K=2,MP1
00380     40 SUMXY(K)=SUMXY(K)+Y(I)*X(I)**(K-1)
00390     50 CONTINUE
00400C
00410C       SET UP THE AUGMENTED MATRIX.
00420C
00430C       THE FIRST ELEMENT OF THE COEFFICIENT ARRAY
00440C
00450        A(1,1)=N
00460C
00470C       ELEMENTS OF THE CONSTANT VECTOR
00480C
00490        DO 70 I=1,MP1
00500        A(I,MP2)=SUMXY(I)
00510C
00520C       OTHER ELEMENTS OF THE COEFFICIENT ARRAY
00530C
00540        DO 60 J=1,MP1
00550        K=I+J-2
00560        IF(K.GT.0) A(I,J)=SUMX(K)
00570     60 CONTINUE
00580     70 CONTINUE
00590        RETURN
00600        END
```

114

SUBROUTINE MATRIX

The variable names used in SUBROUTINE MATRIX(N,X,Y,A,

MP1,MP2,M2,MC) are:

A   -Two-dimensional array containing the elements of the augmented matrix

MC   - Row dimension of the A-matrix as it appears in the calling program

MP1   - Number of normal equations, M+1, where M is the degree of polynomial to be fitted

MP2   - Number of columns in the augmented matrix, M+2

M2   - M x 2

N   - Number of data points

SUMX   - One-dimensional array containing the sums, $\sum x$, $\sum x^2$, $\sum x^3$, ..., $\sum x^{2m}$

SUMXY - One-dimensional array containing the sums, $\sum y$, $\sum xy$, $\sum x^2 y$, ..., $\sum x^m y$

X   - One-dimensional array containing the x-value of the data point

Y   - One-dimensional array containing the y-value of the data point

EXAMPLE 3.2-1.   Choosing among Several Polynomials to Find the One Which Best Represents the Data

Find the polynomial equation which best represents the following set of experimental data points.

x	y
60	1.69
65	1.60
70	1.51
75	1.413
80	1.322
85	1.231
90	1.142
95	1.053
100	0.966
105	0.880
110	0.795
115	0.710
120	0.628

It may be necessary to apply the least squares criterion to several functions to determine which one best represents the data. PROGRAM POLY (see Table 3-6) fits polynomials of the first, second, and third degrees to a set of data points. It calls SUBROUTINE MATRIX to generate the augmented matrix and SUBROUTINE GAUSS to solve the normal equations. Each polynomial is then examined for goodness-of-fit. The sum of the squares of the residuals is calculated for this purpose.

PROGRAM POLY

Description of Input/Output

NDP   -(input) number of data points

X, Y   -(input) one-dimensional arrays containing the x- and
          y-values of the data points

M   - the degree of the polynomial

C   -(output) one-dimensional array containing the coeffi-
          cients of the fitted polynomial

YC   -(output) one-dimensional array containing the fitted
          values of Y

RS   -(intermediate calculation) one-dimensional array
          containing the residuals, Y(I)-YC(I)

SUM   -(output) the sum of the squares of the residuals

PROGRAM POLY was run. The computer printout (see Table 3-7)
reveals that the first degree polynomial is not accurate to
the third decimal place, specifically, the sum of the squares
of the residuals = .52430E-03. The accuracies of both the
second and third degree polynomials are satisfactory. The
polynomial of the third degree is only slightly better than
that of the second degree. Judging from the fact that experi-
mentally determined data are subject to errors, we would choose
a polynomial of the second degree based on both simplicity and
accuracy. Thus we have

$$y = c_1 + c_2 x + c_3 x^2$$

with c_1 = 2.9020, c_2= -0.021334, and c_3 = 0.1980 x 10^{-4}.
The sum of the squares of the residuals = .33752E-04.

Table 3-6. PROGRAM POLY

```
00100          PROGRAM POLY(INPUT,OUTPUT)
00110          DIMENSION X(20),Y(20),A(4,5),C(4),RS(20),YC(20)
00120C
00130C         DATA INPUT
00140C
00150          READ*,NDP
00160          READ*,(X(I),Y(I),I=1,NDP)
00170C
00180C         METHOD OF LEAST SQUARES FIT
00190C
00200          DO 100 M=1,3
00210          MP1=M+1
00220          MP2=M+2
00230          M2=M*2
00240          GO TO (1,2,3),M
00250        1 PRINT 31
00260       31 FORMAT(//" M = 1",5X,"Y(I)=C(1)+C(2)*X")
00270          GO TO 4
00280        2 PRINT 32
00290       32 FORMAT(//" M = 2",5X,"Y(I)=C(1)+C(2)*X+C(3)*X**2")
00300          GO TO 4
00310        3 PRINT 33
00320       33 FORMAT(//," M = 3",5X,
00330+          "Y(I)=C(1)+C(2)*X+C(3)*X**2+C(4)*X**3")
00340C
00350C         CALL SUBROUTINE MATRIX TO SET UP AUGMENTED MATRIX.
00360C
00370        4 CALL MATRIX(NDP,X,Y,A,MP1,MP2,M2,4)
00380C
00390C         CALL SUBROUTINE GAUSS TO SOLVE FOR COEFFICIENTS
00400C         OF FITTED EQUATION.
00410C
00420          CALL GAUSS(A,C,MP1,MP2,4)
00430          PRINT 40,(I,C(I),I=1,MP1)
00440       40 FORMAT(5X,"C(",I2," ) =",E15.5)
00450C
00460C         CHECK GOODNESS-OF-FIT.
00470C
00480          DO 10 I=1,NDP
00490          YC(I)=C(1)
00500          DO 5 J=2,MP1
00510          K=J-1
00520        5 YC(I)=YC(I)+C(J)*X(I)**K
00530       10 RS(I)=Y(I)-YC(I)
00540          SUM=0.
00550          DO 20 I=1,NDP
00560       20 SUM=SUM+RS(I)**2
00570          PRINT 50,SUM
00580       50 FORMAT(1X,"THE SUM OF THE SQUARES OF THE RESIDUALS =",
00590+          E15.5)
00600          PRINT 60,(X(I),Y(I),YC(I),RS(I),I=1,NDP)
00610       60 FORMAT(//10X,"X(I)",11X,"Y(I)",11X,"YC(I)",10X,
00620+          "RS(I)"/(4E15.5))
00630      100 CONTINUE
00640          STOP
00650          END
```

```
00720        SUBROUTINE MATRIX(N,X,Y,A,MP1,MP2,M2,MC)
00730        DIMENSION X(1),Y(1),A(MC,1),SUMX(20),SUMXY(11)
00740        DO 10 K=1,M2
00750     10 SUMX(K)=0.
00760        DO 20 K=1,MP1
00770     20 SUMXY(K)=0.
00780        DO 50 I=1,N
00790        DO 30 K=1,M2
00800     30 SUMX(K)=SUMX(K)+X(I)**K
00810        SUMXY(1)=SUMXY(1)+Y(I)
00820        DO 40 K=2,MP1
00830     40 SUMXY(K)=SUMXY(K)+Y(I)*X(I)**(K-1)
00840     50 CONTINUE
00850        A(1,1)=N
00860        DO 70 I=1,MP1
00870        A(I,MP2)=SUMXY(I)
00880        DO 60 J=1,MP1
00890        K=I+J-2
00900        IF(K.GT.0) A(I,J)=SUMX(K)
00910     60 CONTINUE
00920     70 CONTINUE
00930        RETURN
00940        END


01000        SUBROUTINE GAUSS(A,X,N,NP1,M)
01010        DIMENSION A(M,1),X(1)
01020        DO 100 K=1,N
01030        IF(K.EQ.N) GO TO 30
01040        KP1=K+1
01050        L=K
01060        DO 10 I=KP1,N
01070        IF(ABS(A(I,K)).GT.ABS(A(L,K))) L=I
01080     10 CONTINUE
01090        IF(L.EQ.K) GO TO 30
01100        DO 20 J=K,NP1
01110        C=A(K,J)
01120        A(K,J)=A(L,J)
01130        A(L,J)=C
01140     20 CONTINUE
01150     30 PIVOT=A(K,K)
01160        DO 40 J=K,NP1
01170        A(K,J)=A(K,J)/PIVOT
01180     40 CONTINUE
01190        DO 60 I=1,N
01200        IF(I.EQ.K) GO TO 60
01210        FACTOR=A(I,K)
01220        DO 50 J=K,NP1
01230        A(I,J)=A(I,J)-FACTOR*A(K,J)
01240     50 CONTINUE
01250     60 CONTINUE
01260    100 CONTINUE
01270        DO 200 I=1,N
01280        X(I)=A(I,NP1)
01290    200 CONTINUE
01300        RETURN
01310        END
```

Table 3-7. An application of PROGRAM POLY

DATA INPUT AT TIME OF EXECUTION

```
? 13
? 60., 1.69
? 65., 1.60
? 70., 1.51
? 75., 1.413
? 80., 1.322
? 85., 1.231
? 90., 1.142
? 95., 1.053
? 100., .966
? 105., .880
? 110., .795
? 115., .710
? 120., .628
```

OUTPUT

M = 1   Y(I)=C(1)+C(2)*X
     C(1) =   .27486E+01
     C(2) =   -.17770E-01
THE SUM OF THE SQUARES OF THE RESIDUALS =   .52430E-03

X(I)	Y(I)	YC(I)	RS(I)
.60000E+02	.16900E+01	.16823E+01	.76593E-02
.65000E+02	.16000E+01	.15935E+01	.65110E-02
.70000E+02	.15100E+01	.15046E+01	.53626E-02
.75000E+02	.14130E+01	.14158E+01	-.27857E-02
.80000E+02	.13220E+01	.13269E+01	-.49341E-02
.85000E+02	.12310E+01	.12381E+01	-.70824E-02
.90000E+02	.11420E+01	.11492E+01	-.72308E-02
.95000E+02	.10530E+01	.10604E+01	-.73791E-02
.10000E+03	.96600E+00	.97153E+00	-.55275E-02
.10500E+03	.88000E+00	.88268E+00	-.26758E-02
.11000E+03	.79500E+00	.79382E+00	.11758E-02
.11500E+03	.71000E+00	.70497E+00	.50275E-02
.12000E+03	.62800E+00	.61612E+00	.11879E-01

M = 2   Y(I)=C(1)+C(2)*X+C(3)*X**2
     C(1) =   .29020E+01
     C(2) =   -.21334E-01
     C(3) =   .19800E-04
THE SUM OF THE SQUARES OF THE RESIDUALS =   .33752E-04

X(I)	Y(I)	YC(I)	RS(I)
.60000E+02	.16900E+01	.16932E+01	-.32308E-02
.65000E+02	.16000E+01	.15989E+01	.10659E-02
.70000E+02	.15100E+01	.15056E+01	.43726E-02
.75000E+02	.14130E+01	.14133E+01	-.31069E-03
.80000E+02	.13220E+01	.13220E+01	.15984E-04
.85000E+02	.12310E+01	.12316E+01	-.64735E-03
.90000E+02	.11420E+01	.11423E+01	-.30070E-03
.95000E+02	.10530E+01	.10539E+01	-.94406E-03
.10000E+03	.96600E+00	.96658E+00	-.57742E-03
.10500E+03	.88000E+00	.88020E+00	-.20080E-03
.11000E+03	.79500E+00	.79481E+00	.18581E-03
.11500E+03	.71000E+00	.71042E+00	-.41758E-03
.12000E+03	.62800E+00	.62701E+00	.98901E-03

(continued)

```
M = 3      Y(I)=C(1)+C(2)*X+C(3)*X**2+C(4)*X**3
     C( 1 ) =        .27828E+01
     C( 2 ) =       -.17140E-01
     C( 3 ) =       -.28032E-04
     C( 4 ) =        .17716E-06
THE SUM OF THE SQUARES OF THE RESIDUALS =         .23654E-04
```

X(I)	Y(I)	YC(I)	RS(I)
.60000E+02	.16900E+01	.16918E+01	-.17692E-02
.65000E+02	.16000E+01	.15989E+01	.10659E-02
.70000E+02	.15100E+01	.15064E+01	.35754E-02
.75000E+02	.14130E+01	.14144E+01	-.13736E-02
.80000E+02	.13220E+01	.13229E+01	-.91409E-03
.85000E+02	.12310E+01	.12322E+01	-.11788E-02
.90000E+02	.11420E+01	.11423E+01	-.30070E-03
.95000E+02	.10530E+01	.10534E+01	-.41259E-03
.10000E+03	.96600E+00	.96565E+00	.35265E-03
.10500E+03	.88000E+00	.87914E+00	.86214E-03
.11000E+03	.79500E+00	.79402E+00	.98302E-03
.11500E+03	.71000E+00	.71042E+00	-.41758E-03
.12000E+03	.62800E+00	.62847E+00	-.47253E-03

EXAMPLE 3.2-2.   Pressure-Volume Relation of Steam at Constant

Temperature

The following data is taken from the 1967 ASME Steam Tables.
The temperature is constant at 1000°F.

P (psia)	V (ft^3/lb_m)
30	28.943
40	21.697
50	17.350
60	14.452
70	12.382
80	10.829
90	9.621
100	8.655

Find an expression which represents pressure as a function
of volume.

Since we were successful with polynomial approximation
in Example 3.2-1, we set X = V and Y = P on our first try
and ran PROGRAM POLY. This time we were not so lucky. The
computer printout (see Table 3-8) showed that polynomials of
the first, second, and third degree did not fit the data well.
Refer to Table 3-8. The X(I), Y(I), YC(I), and RS(I) in column
1, 2, 3, and 4 list the values of V, P, P from the fitted polynomial, and the residual, respectively. The sum of the squares
of the residuals is 472.29 for the first degree polynomial,
41.22 for the second degree polynomial, and 2.66 for the third
degree polynomial.

Table 3-8. An ill-suited application of PROGRAM POLY

DATA INPUT AT TIME OF EXECUTION

? 8
? 28.943, 30., 21.697, 40., 17.350, 50., 14.452, 60.
? 12.382, 70., 10.829, 80., 9.621, 90., 8.655, 100.

OUTPUT

```
M = 1     Y(I)=C(1)+C(2)*X
    C( 1 ) =        .11655E+03
    C( 2 ) =       -.33279E+01
THE SUM OF THE SQUARES OF THE RESIDUALS =        .47229E+03
```

X(I)	Y(I)	YC(I)	RS(I)
.28943E+02	.30000E+02	.20234E+02	.97662E+01
.21697E+02	.40000E+02	.44348E+02	-.43476E+01
.17350E+02	.50000E+02	.58814E+02	-.88139E+01
.14452E+02	.60000E+02	.68458E+02	-.84581E+01
.12382E+02	.70000E+02	.75347E+02	-.53468E+01
.10829E+02	.80000E+02	.80515E+02	-.51500E+00
.96210E+01	.90000E+02	.84535E+02	.54649E+01
.86550E+01	.10000E+03	.87750E+02	.12250E+02

```
M = 2     Y(I)=C(1)+C(2)*X+C(3)*X**2
    C( 1 ) =        .17213E+03
    C( 2 ) =       -.10391E+02
    C( 3 ) =        .19090E+00
THE SUM OF THE SQUARES OF THE RESIDUALS =        .41218E+02
```

X(I)	Y(I)	YC(I)	RS(I)
.28943E+02	.30000E+02	.31294E+02	-.12939E+01
.21697E+02	.40000E+02	.36539E+02	.34607E+01
.17350E+02	.50000E+02	.49306E+02	.69363E+00
.14452E+02	.60000E+02	.61826E+02	-.18259E+01
.12382E+02	.70000E+02	.72732E+02	-.27316E+01
.10829E+02	.80000E+02	.81988E+02	-.19875E+01
.96210E+01	.90000E+02	.89824E+02	.17599E+00
.86550E+01	.10000E+03	.96491E+02	.35085E+01

```
M = 3     Y(I)=C(1)+C(2)*X+C(3)*X**2+C(4)*X**3
    C( 1 ) =        .23174E+03
    C( 2 ) =       -.21899E+02
    C( 3 ) =        .86567E+00
    C( 4 ) =       -.12092E-01
THE SUM OF THE SQUARES OF THE RESIDUALS =        .26598E+01
```

X(I)	Y(I)	YC(I)	RS(I)
.28943E+02	.30000E+02	.29907E+02	.92663E-01
.21697E+02	.40000E+02	.40607E+02	-.60709E+00
.17350E+02	.50000E+02	.49220E+02	.77955E+00
.14452E+02	.60000E+02	.59556E+02	.44407E+00
.12382E+02	.70000E+02	.70346E+02	-.34648E+00
.10829E+02	.80000E+02	.80750E+02	-.75030E+00
.96210E+01	.90000E+02	.90406E+02	-.40606E+00
.86550E+01	.10000E+03	.99206E+02	.79365E+00

Next we tried the function

$$y = c_1 + \frac{c_2}{z} + \frac{c_3}{z^2} + \ldots + \frac{c_{m+1}}{z^m} .$$

We let $x = \frac{1}{z}$, and the above equation transformed to

$$y = c_1 + c_2 x + c_3 x^2 + \ldots + c_{m+1} x^m,$$

which is a polynomial of degree m. Thus we may apply the same method that was used in PROGRAM POLY, but with a small change. The new program PROGRAM POLY2 (see Table 3-9) finds the reciprocals of the given x_i input values and then calls SUBROUTINE MATRIX and SUBROUTINE GAUSS in order. PROGRAM POLY2 was run with much better results (see Table 3-10). For m = 2 the fitted equation is

$$y = c_1 + \frac{c_2}{x} + \frac{c_3}{x^2} ,$$

with $c_1 = -0.69503 \times 10^{-2}$, $c_2 = 0.86971 \times 10^3$, and $c_3 = -0.35933 \times 10^2$. The sum of the squares of the residuals is .8507E-05.

We learned from the above example that although polynomials are frequently used in curve fitting, there are times when no polynomial of reasonable degree seems to fit the data. Then other functions should be tried. Theoretically it is possible to find a polynomial function which passes exactly through all of the data points. However, this approach is not always desirable, because the function may represent a curve which oscillates violently about the fitted points. In most instances the degree of a polynomial higher than 3 or 4 is not justified.

Table 3-9. PROGRAM POLY2

```
00100          PROGRAM POLY2(INPUT,OUTPUT)
00110          DIMENSION X(20),Y(20),A(4,5),C(4),RS(20),YC(20)
00120C
00130C         DATA INPUT
00140C
00150          READ*,NDP
00160          READ*,(X(I),Y(I),I=1,NDP)
00170          DO 11 I=1,NDP
00180       11 X(I)=1./X(I)
00190C
00200C         METHOD OF LEAST SQUARES FIT
00210C
00220          DO 100 M=1,3
00230          MP1=M+1
00240          MP2=M+2
00250          M2=M*2
00260          GO TO (1,2,3),M
00270        1 PRINT 31
00280       31 FORMAT(//" M = 1",5X,"Y(I)=C(1)+C(2)/X")
00290          GO TO 4
00300        2 PRINT 32
00310       32 FORMAT(//" M = 2",5X,"Y(I)=C(1)+C(2)/X+C(3)/X**2")
00320          GO TO 4
00330        3 PRINT 33
00340       33 FORMAT(//," M = 3",5X,
00350+         "Y(I)=C(1)+C(2)/X+C(3)/X**2+C(4)/X**3")
00360C
00370C         CALL SUBROUTINE MATRIX TO SET UP AUGMENTED MATRIX.
00380C
00390        4 CALL MATRIX(NDP,X,Y,A,MP1,MP2,M2,4)
00400C
00410C         CALL SUBROUTINE GAUSS TO SOLVE FOR COEFFICIENTS
00420C         OF FITTED EQUATION.
00430C
00440          CALL GAUSS(A,C,MP1,MP2,4)
00450          PRINT 40,(I,C(I),I=1,MP1)
00460       40 FORMAT(5X,"C(",I2," ) =",E15.5)
00470C
00480C         CHECK GOODNESS-OF-FIT.
00490C
00500          DO 10 I=1,NDP
00510          YC(I)=C(1)
00520          DO 5 J=2,MP1
00530          K=J-1
00540        5 YC(I)=YC(I)+C(J)*X(I)**K
00550       10 RS(I)=Y(I)-YC(I)
00560          SUM=0.
00570          DO 20 I=1,NDP
00580       20 SUM=SUM+RS(I)**2
00590          PRINT 50,SUM
00600       50 FORMAT(1X,"THE SUM OF THE SQUARES OF THE RESIDUALS =",
00610+         E15.5)
00620          PRINT 60,(X(I),Y(I),YC(I),RS(I),I=1,NDP)
00630       60 FORMAT(//10X,"X(I)",11X,"Y(I)",11X,"YC(I)",10X,
00640+         "RS(I)"/(4E15.5))
00650      100 CONTINUE
00660          STOP
00670          END
```

```
00730          SUBROUTINE MATRIX(N,X,Y,A,MP1,MP2,M2,MC)
00740          DIMENSION X(1),Y(1),A(MC,1),SUMX(20),SUMXY(11)
00750          DO 10 K=1,M2
00760    10 SUMX(K)=0.
00770          DO 20 K=1,MP1
00780    20 SUMXY(K)=0.
00790          DO 50 I=1,N
00800          DO 30 K=1,M2
00810    30 SUMX(K)=SUMX(K)+X(I)**K
00820          SUMXY(1)=SUMXY(1)+Y(I)
00830          DO 40 K=2,MP1
00840    40 SUMXY(K)=SUMXY(K)+Y(I)*X(I)**(K-1)
00850    50 CONTINUE
00860          A(1,1)=N
00870          DO 70 I=1,MP1
00880          A(I,MP2)=SUMXY(I)
00890          DO 60 J=1,MP1
00900          K=I+J-2
00910          IF(K.GT.0) A(I,J)=SUMX(K)
00920    60 CONTINUE
00930    70 CONTINUE
00940          RETURN
00950          END


01000          SUBROUTINE GAUSS(A,X,N,NP1,M)
01010          DIMENSION A(M,1),X(1)
01020          DO 100 K=1,N
01030          IF(K.EQ.N) GO TO 30
01040          KP1=K+1
01050          L=K
01060          DO 10 I=KP1,N
01070          IF(ABS(A(I,K)).GT.ABS(A(L,K))) L=I
01080    10 CONTINUE
01090          IF(L.EQ.K) GO TO 30
01100          DO 20 J=K,NP1
01110          C=A(K,J)
01120          A(K,J)=A(L,J)
01130          A(L,J)=C
01140    20 CONTINUE
01150    30 PIVOT=A(K,K)
01160          DO 40 J=K,NP1
01170          A(K,J)=A(K,J)/PIVOT
01180    40 CONTINUE
01190          DO 60 I=1,N
01200          IF(I.EQ.K) GO TO 60
01210          FACTOR=A(I,K)
01220          DO 50 J=K,NP1
01230          A(I,J)=A(I,J)-FACTOR*A(K,J)
01240    50 CONTINUE
01250    60 CONTINUE
01260   100 CONTINUE
01270          DO 200 I=1,N
01280          X(I)=A(I,NP1)
01290   200 CONTINUE
01300          RETURN
01310          END
```

126

Table 3-10. An application of PROGRAM POLY2

DATA INPUT AT TIME OF EXECUTION

? 8
? 28.943, 30., 21.697, 40., 17.350, 50., 14.452, 60.
? 12.382, 70., 10.829, 80., 9.621, 90., 8.655, 100.

OUTPUT

M = 1   Y(I)=C(1)+C(2)/X
    C(1) =   .17014E+00
    C(2) =   .86431E+03
THE SUM OF THE SQUARES OF THE RESIDUALS =   .38956E-02

X(I)	Y(I)	YC(I)	RS(I)
.34551E-01	.30000E+02	.30033E+02	-.32789E-01
.46089E-01	.40000E+02	.40006E+02	-.58161E-02
.57637E-01	.50000E+02	.49987E+02	.13452E-01
.69195E-01	.60000E+02	.59976E+02	.23973E-01
.80762E-01	.70000E+02	.69974E+02	.25734E-01
.92345E-01	.80000E+02	.79985E+02	.15040E-01
.10394E+00	.90000E+02	.90006E+02	-.64038E-02
.11554E+00	.10000E+03	.10003E+03	-.33190E-01

M = 2   Y(I)=C(1)+C(2)/X+C(3)/X**2
    C(1) =   -.69503E-02
    C(2) =   .86971E+03
    C(3) =   -.35933E+02
THE SUM OF THE SQUARES OF THE RESIDUALS =   .85070E-05

X(I)	Y(I)	YC(I)	RS(I)
.34551E-01	.30000E+02	.29999E+02	.86791E-03
.46089E-01	.40000E+02	.40001E+02	-.95069E-03
.57637E-01	.50000E+02	.50001E+02	-.91670E-03
.69195E-01	.60000E+02	.60000E+02	-.51746E-04
.80762E-01	.70000E+02	.69998E+02	.16579E-02
.92345E-01	.80000E+02	.79999E+02	.54624E-03
.10394E+00	.90000E+02	.90002E+02	-.16478E-02
.11554E+00	.10000E+03	.10000E+03	.49484E-03

M = 3   Y(I)=C(1)+C(2)/X+C(3)/X**2+C(4)/X**3
    C(1) =   .79152E-03
    C(2) =   .86934E+03
    C(3) =   -.30646E+02
    C(4) =   -.23481E+02
THE SUM OF THE SQUARES OF THE RESIDUALS =   .77215E-05

X(I)	Y(I)	YC(I)	RS(I)
.34551E-01	.30000E+02	.30000E+02	.48585E-03
.46089E-01	.40000E+02	.40001E+02	-.67917E-03
.57637E-01	.50000E+02	.50001E+02	-.53479E-03
.69195E-01	.60000E+02	.60000E+02	.11327E-03
.80762E-01	.70000E+02	.69999E+02	.14957E-02
.92345E-01	.80000E+02	.80000E+02	.16446E-03
.10394E+00	.90000E+02	.90002E+02	-.19217E-02
.11554E+00	.10000E+03	.99999E+02	.87645E-03

127

3.3 Multiple Linear Regression

Frequently experimental data involve more than two variables, and the functions can assume various forms - linear, polynomial, logarithmic, exponential, trigonometric, etc. We consider a linear function of the form

$$y = c_1 + c_2 x_1 + c_3 x_2 + \ldots + c_m x_{m-1} + c_{m+1} x_m. \quad (3.3\text{-}1)$$

The least-squares fit gives us the set of normal equations:

$$
\left.
\begin{aligned}
n c_1 + \left(\sum x_1 \right) c_2 + \ldots + \left(\sum x_m \right) c_{m+1} &= \sum y \\
\left(\sum x_1 \right) c_1 + \left(\sum x_1^2 \right) c_2 + \ldots + \left(\sum x_1 x_m \right) c_{m+1} &= \sum x_1 y \\
\cdots\cdots\cdots\cdots\cdots\cdots\cdots\cdots\cdots\cdots\cdots\cdots\cdots\cdots\cdots\cdots\cdots\cdots \\
\left(\sum x_m \right) c_1 + \left(\sum x_m x_1 \right) c_2 + \ldots + \left(\sum x_m^2 \right) c_{m+1} &= \sum x_m y
\end{aligned}
\right\} \quad (3.3\text{-}2)
$$

For the very simplest model, $m = 1$, Eq. (3.3-1) reduces to the simple linear case discussed under Section 3.1.

We analyze the case for $m = 2$.

$$y = c_1 + c_2 x_1 + c_3 x_2 \qquad (3.3\text{-}3)$$

The normal equations are

$$
\left.
\begin{aligned}
n c_1 + \left(\sum x_1 \right) c_2 + \left(\sum x_2 \right) c_3 &= \sum y \\
\left(\sum x_1 \right) c_1 + \left(\sum x_1^2 \right) c_2 + \left(\sum x_1 x_2 \right) c_3 &= \sum x_1 y \\
\left(\sum x_2 \right) c_1 + \left(\sum x_1 x_2 \right) c_2 + \left(\sum x_2^2 \right) c_3 &= \sum x_2 y
\end{aligned}
\right\} \qquad (3.3\text{-}4)
$$

The augmented matrix is

$$\begin{bmatrix} n & \left(\sum x_1 \right) & \left(\sum x_2 \right) & \left(\sum y \right) \\ \left(\sum x_1 \right) & \left(\sum x_1^2 \right) & \left(\sum x_1 x_2 \right) & \left(\sum x_1 y \right) \\ \left(\sum x_2 \right) & \left(\sum x_1 x_2 \right) & \left(\sum x_2^2 \right) & \left(\sum x_2 y \right) \end{bmatrix} \qquad (3.3\text{-}5)$$

The first element a_{11} is n. The following elements are formed by summations.

$$a_{12} = \sum x_1 \qquad\qquad a_{13} = \sum x_2$$

$$a_{14} = \sum y \qquad\qquad a_{22} = \sum x_1^2$$

$$a_{23} = \sum x_1 x_2 \qquad\qquad a_{24} = \sum x_1 y$$

$$a_{33} = \sum x_2^2 \qquad\qquad a_{34} = \sum x_2 y$$

The remaining elements are obtained from the identities

$$a_{21} = a_{12}, \qquad a_{31} = a_{13}, \qquad a_{32} = a_{23}.$$

Then Eq. (3.3-4) may be solved by the Gauss-Jordan method described in Section 2.2 to obtain c_1, c_2, and c_3.

Subprogram SUBROUTINE COEFF (see Table 3-11) was written to generate the elements of the augmented matrix of Eq. (3.3-5).

Table 3-11. SUBROUTINE COEFF

```
00100      SUBROUTINE COEFF(N,X1,X2,Y,A)
00110C
00120C     THIS PROGRAM GENERATES THE AUGMENTED MATRIX OF THE
00130C     THREE NORMAL EQUATIONS FOR MULTIPLE LINEAR REGRESSION
00140C     OF Y=C1+C2*X1+C3*X2.
00150C
00160      DIEMNSION X1(1),X2(1),Y(1),A(3,4)
00170C
00180C     CLEAR ELEMENTS OF ARRAY A.
00190C
00200      DO 10 I=1,3
00210      DO 10 J=1,4
00220   10 A(I,J)=0.
00230C
00240C     THE FIRST ELEMENT OF ARRAY A
00250C
00260      A(1,1)=N
00270C
00280C     COMPUTE THE SUMMATIONS AND LOAD THE A-MATRIX
00290C     AT THE PROPER POSITIONS.
00300C
00310      DO 20 I=1,N
00320      A(1,2)=A(1,2)+X1(I)
00330      A(1,3)=A(1,3)+X2(I)
00340      A(1,4)=A(1,4)+Y(I)
00350      A(2,2)=A(2,2)+X1(I)*X1(I)
00360      A(2,3)=A(2,3)+X1(I)*X2(I)
00370      A(2,4)=A(2,4)+X1(I)*Y(I)
00380      A(3,3)=A(3,3)+X2(I)*X2(I)
00390   20 A(3,4)=A(3,4)+X2(I)*Y(I)
00400C
00410C     THE REMAINING ELEMENTS ARE OBTAINED FROM THE
00420C     IDENTITIES.
00430C
00440      A(2,1)=A(1,2)
00450      A(3,1)=A(1,3)
00460      A(3,2)=A(2,3)
00470      RETURN
00480      END
```

EXAMPLE 3.3-1. <u>A Heat Transfer Correlation</u>

The following equation has been derived by dimensional analysis to correlate the heat transfer to a fluid flowing inside a tube in turbulent flow.

$$Nu = \alpha\, Re^{\beta}\, Pr^{\gamma} \qquad (3.3\text{-}6)$$

where Nu = Nusselt number,

   Re = Reynolds number,

   Pr = Prandtl number,

   α , β , γ = constants.

Fit Eq. (3.3-6) to the following experimental data and find the constants α , β , and γ .

Nu	Re	Pr
426	131200	2.7
375	58000	10.0
340	39150	17.7
210	17160	25.5
265	18250	41.3

Taking logarithms of both members of Eq. (3.3-6), we have

$$\ln Nu = \ln\alpha + \beta \ln Re + \gamma \ln Pr. \qquad (3.3\text{-}7)$$

Let

$$z = \ln Nu, \quad x = \ln Re, \quad y = \ln Pr,$$
$$c_1 = \ln\alpha, \quad c_2 = \beta, \quad c_3 = \gamma . \qquad (3.3\text{-}8)$$

Substituting Eq. (3.3-8) into (3.3-7), we obtain

$$z = c_1 + c_2 x + c_3 y. \qquad (3.3\text{-}9)$$

131

The method of multiple linear regression can be applied. PROGRAM DA (see Table 3-12) was developed for solving Example 3.3-1.

PROGRAM DA

Description of Input/Output

N   -(input) number of data points

NU,RE,PR -(input) one-dimensional arrays containing the
            Nusselt, Reynolds, and Prandtl numbers, respectively

X,Y,Z   -(intermediate calculation) one-dimensional arrays

A   -(intermediate calculation) two-dimensional array
            containing the elements of the augmented matrix

C   -(intermediate calculation) one-dimensional array
            containing the solution vector of the normal equations

ALPHA,BETA,GAMMA - (output) the fitted coefficients

CNU   -(output) one-dimensional array containing the fitted
            values of the Nusselt number

Input data must be read in the following order:

    N,(NU(I),RE(I),PR(I),I=1,N)

Following the READ statement, the main program, PROGRAM DA, calls SUBROUTINE COEFF to generate the augmented matrix and SUBROUTINE GAUSS to solve for the coefficients. Finally, the main program calculates CNU, the fitted Nusselt number, to determine the goodness-of-fit.

Table 3-12. PROGRAM DA

```
00100          PROGRAM DA(INPUT,OUTPUT)
00110          REAL NU
00120          DIMENSION NU(10),RE(10),PR(10),X(10),Y(10),Z(10),
00130+         A(3,4),C(3),CNU(10)
00140C
00150C         DATA INPUT
00160C
00170          READ*,N
00180          DO 10 I=1,N
00190          READ*,NU(I),RE(I),PR(I)
00200          X(I)=ALOG(RE(I))
00210          Y(I)=ALOG(PR(I))
00220       10 Z(I)=ALOG(NU(I))
00230C
00240C         CALL CUBROUTINE COEFF AND SUBROUTINE GAUSS TO
00250C         PERFORM MULTIPLE LINEAR REGRESSION.
00260C
00270          CALL COEFF(N,X,Y,Z,A)
00280          CALL GAUSS(A,C,3,4,3)
00290C
00300C         OUTPUT
00310C
00320          ALPHA=EXP(C(1))
00330          BETA=C(2)
00340          GAMMA=C(3)
00350          PRINT 15,ALPHA,BETA,GAMMA
00360       15 FORMAT(//" THE FITTED EQUATION IS"/
00370+         "NU =(",F10.5," )*RE**(",F10.5,
00380+         ")*PR**(",F10.5,")")
00390          DO 20 I=1,N
00400       20 CNU(I)=ALPHA*RE(I)**BETA*PR(I)**GAMMA
00410          PRINT 30
00420       30 FORMAT(//"         NU(I)         RE(I)         ",
00430+         "PR(I)        CNU(I)")
00440          PRINT 40,(NU(I),RE(I),PR(I),CNU(I),I=1,N)
00450       40 FORMAT(F10.1,F13.0,2F10.1)
00460          STOP
00470          END


00500          SUBROUTINE COEFF(N,X1,X2,Y,A)
00510          DIMENSION X1(1),X2(1),Y(1),A(3,4)
00520          DO 10 I=1,3
00530          DO 10 J=1,4
00540       10 A(I,J)=0.
00550          A(1,1)=N
00560          DO 20 I=1,N
00570          A(1,2)=A(1,2)+X1(I)
00580          A(1,3)=A(1,3)+X2(I)
00590          A(1,4)=A(1,4)+Y(I)
00600          A(2,2)=A(2,2)+X1(I)*X1(I)
00610          A(2,3)=A(2,3)+X1(I)*X2(I)
00620          A(2,4)=A(2,4)+X1(I)*Y(I)
00630          A(3,3)=A(3,3)+X2(I)*X2(I)
00640       20 A(3,4)=A(3,4)+X2(I)*Y(I)
00650          A(2,1)=A(1,2)
00660          A(3,1)=A(1,3)
00670          A(3,2)=A(2,3)
00680          RETURN
00690          END
```

133

```
00750          SUBROUTINE GAUSS(A,X,N,NP1,M)
00760          DIMENSION A(M,1),X(1)
00770          DO 100 K=1,N
00780          IF(K.EQ.N) GO TO 30
00790          KP1=K+1
00800          L=K
00810          DO 10 I=KP1,N
00820          IF(ABS(A(I,K)).GT.ABS(A(L,K))) L=I
00830       10 CONTINUE
00840          IF(L.EQ.K) GO TO 30
00850          DO 20 J=K,NP1
00860          C=A(K,J)
00870          A(K,J)=A(L,J)
00880          A(L,J)=C
00890       20 CONTINUE
00900       30 PIVOT=A(K,K)
00910          DO 40 J=K,NP1
00920          A(K,J)=A(K,J)/PIVOT
00930       40 CONTINUE
00940          DO 60 I=1,N
00950          IF(I.EQ.K) GO TO 60
00960          FACTOR=A(I,K)
00970          DO 50 J=K,NP1
00980          A(I,J)=A(I,J)-FACTOR*A(K,J)
00990       50 CONTINUE
01000       60 CONTINUE
01010      100 CONTINUE
01020          DO 200 I=1,N
01030          X(I)=A(I,NP1)
01040      200 CONTINUE
01050          RETURN
01060          END
```

Table 3-13. An application of PROGRAM DA

DATA INPUT AT TIME OF EXECUTION

? 5
? 426., 131200., 2.7
? 375., 58000., 10.
? 340., 39150., 17.7
? 210., 17160., 25.5
? 265., 18250., 41.3

OUTPUT

THE FITTED EQUATION IS
NU =(.03941)*RE**(.75679)*PR**(.37163)

NU(I)	RE(I)	PR(I)	CNU(I)
426.0	131200.	2.7	425.7
375.0	58000.	10.0	373.4
340.0	39150.	17.7	342.9
210.0	17160.	25.5	210.4
265.0	18250.	41.3	263.6

For the given data the solution set is

$$ALPHA = 0.03941,$$

$$BETA = 0.75679,$$

$$GAMMA = 0.37163.$$

A comparison of the values in column 1, NU(I), and in column 4, CNU(I), of the output printout (see Table 3-13) shows that the fit is reasonably good.

EXAMPLE 3.3-2. The Antoine Equation

Rework Example 3.1-2, but fit the Antoine equation to the data.

In Example 3.1-2 an empirical equation of the form

$$\log_{10} P = A + \frac{B}{T}$$

was used to represent vapor pressure of benzene as a function of temperature. This equation is useful for many purposes, but it is not very accurate. A more satisfactory one is the Antoine equation, which has the form

$$\log_{10} P = A - \frac{B}{C + t}, \qquad (3.3\text{-}10)$$

where P = vapor pressure,

   t = temperature,

   A, B, and C are the Antoine constants.

In order to perform the least squares fit, Eq. (3.3-10) must be linearized. A brief derivation follows.

Multiplying Eq.(3.3-10) by (C + t) and rearranging, we have

$$\log_{10} P = (A - \frac{B}{C}) + \frac{A}{C} t - \frac{1}{C} (t \log_{10} P). \qquad (3.3-11)$$

Letting

$$
\left.
\begin{aligned}
y &= \log_{10} P, \\
x_1 &= t, \\
x_2 &= t \log_{10} P, \\
\alpha &= A - B/C, \\
\beta &= A/C, \\
\gamma &= -1/C,
\end{aligned}
\right\} \qquad (3.3-12)
$$

we have

$$y = \alpha + \beta x_1 + \gamma x_2. \qquad (3.3-13)$$

Eq. (3.3-13) is of the same form as Eq. (3.3-3). SUBROUTINE COEFF can be used to generate the augmented matrix of the normal equations and SUBROUTINE GAUSS to solve for α, β, and γ. The Antoine constants are obtained from α, β, and γ as follows.

$$
\begin{aligned}
A &= -\beta/\gamma, \\
B &= (\alpha + \beta/\gamma)/\gamma, \qquad (3.3-14) \\
C &= -1/\gamma.
\end{aligned}
$$

PROGRAM ANTOINE (see Table 3-14) was developed, based on that procedure. After the Antoine constants are obtained the main program calculates the fitted vapor pressures to determine the goodness-of-fit.

PROGRAM ANTOINE

Description of Input/Output

N   -(input) number of data points

T   -(input) one-dimensional array containing the temper-
        atures

P   -(input) one-dimensional array containing the pressures

Y,X1,X2-(intermediate calculations) one-dimensional arrays

CC   -(intermediate calculation) one-dimensional array
        containing the values of α, β, and γ of Eq. (3.3-13)

AM   -(intermediate calculation) two-dimensional array
        containing the elements of the augmented matrix

A,B,C -(output) the Antoine constants

PCAL   -(output) one-dimensional array containing the fitted
        vapor pressures

        PROGRAM ANTOINE was run to solve Example 3.3-2.   The

values of the Antoine constants are (see Table 3-15):

        A = 6.8792,   B = 1196.42,   C = 219.12.

A comparison of the fitted vapor pressures indicates that the

Antoine equation fits the data better than the empirical

equation of Example 3.1-2.

T, $^\circ$C	P, mm Hg	PCAL (Antoine equation)	PCAL (Example 3.1-2)
7.60	40.00	40.02	40.71
15.40	60.00	59.94	60.00
26.10	100.00	100.08	98.84
42.20	200.00	199.95	196.52
60.60	400.00	400.02	397.41
80.10	760.00	760.00	773.72

138

Table 3-14. PROGRAM ANTOINE

```
00100          PROGRAM ANTOINE(INPUT,OUTPUT)
00110          DIMENSION T(10),P(10),AM(3,4),CC(3),PCAL(10),
00120+         X1(10),X2(10),Y(10)
00130          EQUIVALENCE (T,X1)
00140C
00150C         DATA INPUT
00160C
00170          READ*,N
00180          READ*,(T(I),P(I),I=1,N)
00190          DO 10 I=1,N
00200          Y(I)=ALOG10(P(I))
00210      10 X2(I)=T(I)*Y(I)
00220C
00230C         CALL SUBROUTINE COEFF TO SET UP THE AUGMENTED MATRIX.
00240C
00250          CALL COEFF(N,X1,X2,Y,AM)
00260C
00270C         CALL SUBROUTINE GAUSS TO SOLVE THE NORMAL EQUATIONS.
00280C
00290          CALL GAUSS(AM,CC,3,4,3)
00300C
00310C         OUTPUT PRINTS THE VALUES OF THE ANTOINE CONSTANTS
00320C         AND THE FITTED VALUES OF P VS. T.
00330C
00340          A=-CC(2)/CC(3)
00350          B=(CC(1)+CC(2)/CC(3))/CC(3)
00360          C=-1./CC(3)
00370          DO 1 I=1,N
00380       1 PCAL(I)=10.**(A-B/(C+T(I)))
00390          PRINT 2,A,B,C
00400       2 FORMAT(//6X,"A",9X,"B",9X,"C"/F10.4,2F10.2)
00410          PRINT 3
00420       3 FORMAT(//6X,"T",9X,"P",8X,"PCAL")
00430          PRINT 4,(T(I),P(I),PCAL(I),I=1,N)
00440       4 FORMAT(3F10.2)
00450          STOP
00460          END


00500          SUBROUTINE COEFF(N,X1,X2,Y,A)
00510          DIMENSION X1(1),X2(1),Y(1),A(3,4)
00520          DO 10 I=1,3
00530          DO 10 J=1,4
00540      10 A(I,J)=0.
00550          A(1,1)=N
00560          DO 20 I=1,N
00570          A(1,2)=A(1,2)+X1(I)
00580          A(1,3)=A(1,3)+X2(I)
00590          A(1,4)=A(1,4)+Y(I)
00600          A(2,2)=A(2,2)+X1(I)*X1(I)
00610          A(2,3)=A(2,3)+X1(I)*X2(I)
00620          A(2,4)=A(2,4)+X1(I)*Y(I)
00630          A(3,3)=A(3,3)+X2(I)*X2(I)
00640      20 A(3,4)=A(3,4)+X2(I)*Y(I)
00650          A(2,1)=A(1,2)
00660          A(3,1)=A(1,3)
00670          A(3,2)=A(2,3)
00680          RETURN
00690          END
```

139

```
00750         SUBROUTINE GAUSS(A,X,N,NP1,M)
00760         DIMENSION A(M,1),X(1)
00770         DO 100 K=1,N
00780         IF(K.EQ.N) GO TO 30
00790         KP1=K+1
00800         L=K
00810         DO 10 I=KP1,N
00820         IF(ABS(A(I,K)).GT.ABS(A(L,K))) L=I
00830      10 CONTINUE
00840         IF(L.EQ.K) GO TO 30
00850         DO 20 J=K,NP1
00860         C=A(K,J)
00870         A(K,J)=A(L,J)
00880         A(L,J)=C
00890      20 CONTINUE
00900      30 PIVOT=A(K,K)
00910         DO 40 J=K,NP1
00920         A(K,J)=A(K,J)/PIVOT
00930      40 CONTINUE
00940         DO 60 I=1,N
00950         IF(I.EQ.K) GO TO 60
00960         FACTOR=A(I,K)
00970         DO 50 J=K,NP1
00980         A(I,J)=A(I,J)-FACTOR*A(K,J)
00990      50 CONTINUE
01000      60 CONTINUE
01010     100 CONTINUE
01020         DO 200 I=1,N
01030         X(I)=A(I,NP1)
01040     200 CONTINUE
01050         RETURN
01060         END
```

Table 3-15. An application of PROGRAM ANTOINE

DATA INPUT AT TIME OF EXECUTION

? 6
? 7.6, 40.
? 15.4, 60.
? 26.1, 100.
? 42.2, 200.
? 60.6, 400.,
? 80.1, 760.

OUTPUT

A	B	C
6.8792	1196.42	219.12

T	P	PCAL
7.60	40.00	40.02
15.40	60.00	59.94
26.10	100.00	100.08
42.20	200.00	199.95
60.60	400.00	400.02
80.10	760.00	760.00

3-A. The following data of the viscosities of benzene at various temperatures are taken from the Handbook of Chemistry and Physics (Weast, 1968).

Temperature, °C	Viscosity, c.p.
0	.912
10	.758
20	.652
30	.564
40	.503
50	.442
60	.392
70	.358
80	.329

Fit a polynomial function of the following form to the experimental data.

$$y = C_1 + C_2 x + \ldots + C_{m+1} x^m, \qquad (3.A-1)$$

where x = temperature,

y = viscosity,

C_1, C_2, ... = constants,

m = the degree of the polynomial.

Work the problem for $m = 2$ and 3.

Answers:

For $m = 2$: $C_1 = .89499$, $C_2 = -.13057 \times 10^{-1}$, $C_3 = .76255 \times 10^{-4}$.

For $m = 3$: $C_1 = .90749$, $C_2 = -.15751 \times 10^{-1}$, $C_3 = .16555 \times 10^{-3}$, $C_4 = -.74411 \times 10^{-6}$.

The fitted viscosities are:

.895 .772 .664 .572 .495 .433 .386 .355 .338 (for $m = 2$),
.907 .766 .653 .564 .495 .441 .398 .361 .326 (for $m = 3$).

3-B. It is known that the variation of the viscosity of liquids
with temperature may be represented quite well by

$$\ln \mu = A + B/T, \qquad\qquad (3.B-1)$$

where μ = viscosity,

T = absolute temperature ($^\circ$K = $^\circ$C + 273.15),

A, B = constants.

Fit Eq. (3.B-1) to the data of Prob. 3-A.

Answers:

A = -4.6109,   B = .12285x10^4.

The fitted viscosities are:

.893 .762 .657 .572 .503 .445 .397 .357 .322.

Notice that Eq. (3.B-1) has only two constants, yet its
accuracy is comparable to the accuracies of polynomials
having three or four constants.

3-C. The following vapor-liquid equilibrium ratio constants of
n-hexane at 50 psia are taken from the generalized correlation
charts by DePriester (1953).

Temperature, $^\circ$F	K = y/x
150	.298
200	.60
250	1.10
300	1.77
350	2.65

Using the method of least squares, fit polynomials of second
and third degrees to the data.

Answers:

    (a) $K = a + bT + cT^2$ (T in °F),

        $a = .52503$, $b = -.71949 \times 10^{-2}$, $c = .37886 \times 10^{-4}$.

        The fitted K-values are:

        .298 .601 1.094 1.776 2.648.

    (b) $K = a + bT + cT^2 + dT^3$ (T in °F),

        $a = .41703$, $b = -.57629 \times 10^{-2}$, $c = .31886 \times 10^{-4}$,

        $d = .800 \times 10^{-8}$.

        The fitted K-values are:

        .297 .604 1.094 1.774 2.649.

3-D. Rework Prob. 3-C. Fit the equation

$$\ln K = a + bT + cT^2 \text{ (T in °F)} \qquad (3.\text{D-1})$$

to the data.

Answers:

        $a = -3.9300$, $b = .21233 \times 10^{-1}$, $c = -.20657 \times 10^{-4}$.

        The fitted K-values are:

        .298 .601 1.091 1.787 2.641.

3-E. In Example 3.3-2 we have shown how the Antoine equation can be linearized. If the concept of best fit by the method of least squares is applied directly, we will minimize the sum of the squares of the deviations as follows:

$$E = \sum_{1}^{n} \left[\log_{10} P - \left(A - \frac{B}{C + t} \right) \right]^2 = \text{minimum}, \quad (3.E\text{-}1)$$

It follows from (3.E-1) that

$$\frac{\partial E}{\partial A} = 0, \quad \frac{\partial E}{\partial B} = 0, \quad \text{and} \quad \frac{\partial E}{\partial C} = 0.$$

Three highly nonlinear normal equations result.

$$\left. \begin{array}{l} \sum(\log_{10} P) = nA - B \sum \left(\frac{1}{C + t} \right), \\[2ex] \sum \left(\frac{1}{C + t} \right)(\log_{10} P) = A \sum \left(\frac{1}{C + t} \right) - B \sum \left(\frac{1}{C + t} \right)^2, \\[2ex] \sum \left(\frac{1}{C + t} \right)^2 (\log_{10} P) = A \sum \left(\frac{1}{C + t} \right)^2 - B \sum \left(\frac{1}{C + t} \right)^3. \end{array} \right\} \quad (3.E\text{-}2)$$

Letting $y = \log_{10} P$ and $x = \frac{1}{C + t}$, we have

$$\sum y = \quad nA - B \sum x, \qquad\qquad\qquad (3.E\text{-}3a)$$

$$\sum xy = A \sum x - B \sum x^2, \qquad\qquad\qquad (3.E\text{-}3b)$$

$$\sum x^2 y = A \sum x^2 - B \sum x^3. \qquad\qquad\qquad (3.E\text{-}3c)$$

Solving (3.E-3a) and (3.E-3b) simultaneously for A and B in terms of the third coefficient C, we obtain

$$A = \frac{\left(\sum y \right)\left(\sum x^2 \right) - \left(\sum x \right)\left(\sum xy \right)}{n\left(\sum x^2 \right) - \left(\sum x \right)^2}, \qquad\qquad (3.E\text{-}4a)$$

$$B = \frac{\left(\sum x \right)\left(\sum y \right) - n\left(\sum xy \right)}{n\left(\sum x^2 \right) - \left(\sum x \right)^2}. \qquad\qquad (3.E\text{-}4b)$$

When Eqs. (3.E-4a) and (3.E-4b) are substituted into (3.E-3c) to eliminate A and B, the resulting equation is a function of C only.

$$f(C)$$

$$= \sum x^2 y$$

$$- \frac{\left(\sum x^2\right)\left[\left(\sum y\right)\left(\sum x^2\right) - \left(\sum x\right)\left(\sum xy\right)\right] - \left(\sum x^3\right)\left[\left(\sum x\right)\left(\sum y\right) - n\left(\sum xy\right)\right]}{n\left(\sum x^2\right) - \left(\sum x\right)^2}$$

$$= 0. \tag{3.E-5}$$

We may resort to an iterative method (such as the method of regula falsi described in chapter one) to solve Eq. (3.E-5). For the initial approximation we set $C = 230$, following the vapor pressure equation of Calingaert and Davis (1925). As soon as the numerical value of C is established, the values of A and B are obtained from Eqs. (3.E-4a) and (3.E-4b).

Rework Example 3.3-2, following the method outlined above. Compare the results with those of Example 3.3-2.

Answers:

$A = 6.8789$, $B = 1196.247$, $C = 219.105$.

The fitted vapor pressure data vs. temperature are:

T, °C	v.p., mm Hg
7.60	40.02
15.40	59.94
26.10	100.08
42.20	199.95
60.60	400.02
80.10	759.99

The results are essentially the same as those of Example 3.3-2.

Chapter 4

Numerical Integration and Differentiation

4.1 Introduction

Numerical integration is commonly used to solve problems
when integration by analytical methods becomes difficult or
impossible. I⁺ is relatively easy to carry out a numerical
integration. In two dimensions the technique involves the
estimation of the area under a curve. Two schemes to approximate the area, one by the trapezoid rule and the other by the
Simpson's rule, will be discussed.

4.2 Numerical Integration by the Trapezoid Rule

The trapezoid rule is one of the simplest formulas for
numerical integration. It involves the following steps:

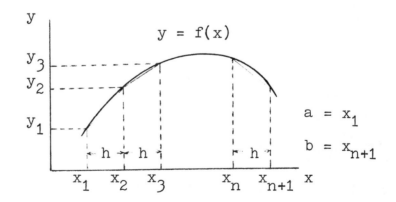

Figure 4-1. Numerical integration by the
trapezoid rule

(a) As shown in Figure 4-1, the interval of integration from a to b is divided into n equal subintervals. The width of a subinterval is given by $h = (b - a)/n$.

(b) The area of each subinterval is approximated by that of a trapezoid.

(c) The total area is the sum of the areas of the n trapezoids and approximates the value of the integral.

$$\text{Area} = \int_a^b f(x)\ dx$$

$$\approx h\left[\left(\frac{y_1 + y_2}{2}\right) + \left(\frac{y_2 + y_3}{2}\right) + \ldots + \left(\frac{y_n + y_{n+1}}{2}\right)\right]$$

$$\approx h\left[\left(\frac{y_1 + y_{n+1}}{2}\right) + (y_2 + y_3 + \ldots + y_n)\right]$$

$$\approx h\left[\frac{y_1 + y_{n+1}}{2} + \sum_{i=2}^{n} y_i\right], \qquad (4.2\text{-}1)$$

where $y_1 = f(a)$,

$\quad y_2 = f(a + h)$,

$\quad y_3 = f(a + 2h)$,

$\quad \ldots\ldots\ldots\ldots\ldots$,

$\quad y_n = f\left[a + (n-1)h\right]$,

$\quad y_{n+1} = f(b)$.

The approximate error of the trapezoid rule is

$$-\frac{(b - a)^3}{12n^2}\ f''(\xi), \qquad a < \xi < b.$$

148

EXAMPLE 4.2-1. The Trapezoid Rule

Evaluate the following integral pertinent to the Maxwell-
Boltzman distribution by the trapezoid rule.

$$\int_0^x x^3 e^{-x^2} dx$$

for x = 1.0. Evaluate, using 10, 100, and 1000 subintervals.

PROGRAM TRAPZD

Description of Input/Output

A   -(input) the lower limit of integration

B   -(input) the upper limit of integration

N   -(input) the number of subintervals

H   -(intermediate calculation) the width of a subinterval

AREA   -(output) the approximate value of the integral

PROGRAM TRAPZD (see Table 4-1) was run first for n = 10.
The approximate value of the integral was 0.13243 (see Table 4-2).
It was rerun for n = 100 and 1000. The approximate value was
0.13212 in both cases. Normally we would expect increased
accuracy with an increased number of subintervals. However, it
must be pointed out that sometimes decreasing h produces a less
accurate result. In our case 0.13212 was the better approximation.

Table 4-1. PROGRAM TRAPZD

```
00100      PROGRAM TRAPZD(INPUT,OUTPUT)
00110C
00120C     THIS PROGRAM PERFORMS NUMERICAL INTEGRATION BY
00130C     THE TRAPEZOID RULE.
00140C
00150C     DEFINE FUNCTION
00160C
00170      F(X)=X**3*EXP(-X**2)
00180C
00190C     READ IN LOWER AND UPPER LIMITS OF INTEGRATION
00200C     AND THE NUMBER OF SUBINTERVALS.
00210C
00220      READ*,A,B,N
00230      H=(B-A)/N
00240C
00250C     INTEGRATION BY THE TRAPEZOID RULE
00260C
00270      SUM=0.
00280      X=A+H
00290      DO 10 I=2,N
00300      SUM=SUM+F(X)
00310   10 X=X+H
00320      AREA=H*((F(A)+F(B))/2.+SUM)
00330C
00340C     OUTPUT
00350C
00360      PRINT 20,A,B,N
00370   20 FORMAT(//5X,"A =",F10.4,5X,"B =",F10.4,5X," N =",I10)
00380      PRINT 30,AREA
00390   30 FORMAT(//10X,"VALUE OF INTEGRAL =",E15.5)
00400      STOP
00410      END
```

Table 4-2. An application of PROGRAM TRAPZD

DATA INPUT AT TIME OF EXECUTION

? 0., 1., 10

OUTPUT

    A =   0.0000   B =   1.0000   N =   10

    VALUE OF INTEGRAL =   .13243E+00

DATA INPUT AT TIME OF EXECUTION

? 0., 1., 100

OUTPUT

    A =   0.0000   B =   1.0000   N =   100

    VALUE OF INTEGRAL =   .13212E+00

DATA INPUT AT TIME OF EXECUTION

? 0., 1., 1000

OUTPUT

    A =   0.0000   B =   1.0000   N =   1000

    VALUE OF INTEGRAL =   .13212E+00

4.3 Numerical Integration by Simpson's Rule

A somewhat better method of numerical integration is Simpson's rule, which is one of the most widely used. It assumes that the curve can be represented by a cubic equation of the form

$$y = a_0 + a_1 x + a_2 x^2 + a_3 x^3. \qquad (4.3\text{-}1)$$

The area contained in the two adjacent strips in the interval x_1 to x_3 in Figure 4-1 is

$$A_1 = \int_{x_1}^{x_3} y \, dx$$

$$= \int_{x_1}^{x_3} (a_0 + a_1 x + a_2 x^2 + a_3 x^3) \, dx$$

$$= a_0(x_3 - x_1) + \frac{a_1}{2}(x_3^2 - x_1^2) + \frac{a_2}{3}(x_3^3 - x_1^3) + \frac{a_3}{4}(x_3^4 - x_1^4). \qquad (4.3\text{-}2)$$

Noting that $x_2 = x_1 + h$ and $x_3 = x_1 + 2h$, we have

$$A_1 = h\left[2a_0 + a_1(2x_1 + 2h) + a_2\left(2x_1^2 + 4x_1 h + \frac{8h^2}{3}\right) + \right.$$

$$\left. a_3(2x_1^3 + 6x_1^2 h + 8x_1 h^2 + 4h^3)\right]. \qquad (4.3\text{-}3)$$

Since

$$
\left.
\begin{aligned}
y_1 &= a_0 + a_1 x_1 + a_2 x_1^2 + a_3 x_1^3 \\
y_2 &= a_0 + a_1 x_2 + a_2 x_2^2 + a_3 x_2^3 \\
&= a_0 + a_1(x_1 + h) + a_2(x_1 + h)^2 + a_3(x_1 + h)^3 \\
y_3 &= a_0 + a_1 x_3 + a_2 x_3^2 + a_3 x_3^3 \\
&= a_0 + a_1(x_1 + 2h) + a_2(x_1 + 2h)^2 + a_3(x_1 + 2h)^3,
\end{aligned}
\right\} \qquad (4.3\text{-}4)
$$

152

we have

$$\frac{h}{3}(y_1+4y_2+y_3) = h\left[2a_0 + a_1(2x_1+2h) + a_2(2x_1^2+4x_1h+\frac{8h^2}{3}) + \right.$$

$$\left. a_3(2x_1^3+6x_1^2h+8x_1h^2+4h^3)\right]. \qquad (4.3\text{-}5)$$

Therefore

$$A_1 = \frac{h}{3}(y_1+4y_2+y_3). \qquad (4.3\text{-}6)$$

If the interval from x = a to x = b is divided into n (even number) equal strips, there are n/2 such areas. Summing these areas, we obtain

$$\int_a^b y\,dx = \sum_{i=1}^{n/2} A_i$$

$$= \frac{h}{3}\left[(y_1+4y_2+y_3) + (y_3+4y_4+y_5) + \dots + \right.$$

$$\left. (y_{n-1}+4y_n+y_{n+1})\right]$$

$$= \frac{h}{3}(y_1 + 4\sum_{i=2,4,6,8,\dots}^{n} y_i + 2\sum_{i=3,5,7,\dots}^{n-1} y_i +$$

$$y_{n+1}). \qquad (4.3\text{-}7)$$

Simpson's rule gives the exact value of a definite integral providing the integrand is a polynomial of first, second, or third degree.

The approximate error of Simpson's rule is

$$-\frac{(b-a)^5}{180n^4} f^{(4)}(\xi), \quad a < \xi < b.$$

EXAMPLE 4.3-1. Simpson's Rule

Rework Example 4.2-1, using Simpson's rule.

Table 4-3. PROGRAM SIMPSON

```
00100      PROGRAM SIMPSON(INPUT,OUTPUT)
00110C
00120C     THIS PROGRAM PERFORMS NUMERICAL INTEGRATION BY
00130C     THE SIMPSON'S RULE.
00140C
00150C     DEFINE FUNCTION
00160C
00170      F(X)=X**3*EXP(-X**2)
00180C
00190C     READ IN LOWER AND UPPER LIMITS OF INTEGRATION
00200C     AND THE NUMBER OF SUBINTERVALS.
00210C
00220      READ*,A,B,N
00230      H=(B-A)/N
00240C
00250C     INTEGRATION BY SIMPSON'S RULE
00260C
00270      SUM2=0.
00280      SUM3=0.
00290      DO 10 I=2,N,2
00300      SUM2=SUM2+F(A+(I-1)*H)
00310      IF(I.EQ.N) GO TO 10
00320      SUM3=SUM3+F(A+I*H)
00330   10 CONTINUE
00340      AREA=H/3.*(F(A)+4.*SUM2+2.*SUM3+F(B))
00350C
00360C     OUTPUT
00370C
00380      PRINT 20,A,B,N
00390   20 FORMAT(//5X,"A =",F10.4,5X,"B =",F10.4,5X,"N =",I10)
00400      PRINT 30,AREA
00410   30 FORMAT(//10X,"VALUE OF INTEGRAL =",E15.5)
00420      STOP
00430      END
```

Table 4-4. An application of PROGRAM SIMPSON

DATA INPUT AT TIME OF EXECUTION

? 0., 1., 10

OUTPUT

A =   0.0000   B =   1.0000   N =   10

        VALUE OF INTEGRAL =   .13212E+00

DATA INPUT AT TIME OF EXECUTION

? 0., 1., 100

OUTPUT

A =   0.0000   B =   1.0000   N =   100

        VALUE OF INTEGRAL =   .13212E+00

PROGRAM SIMPSON

<u>Description of Input/Output</u>

Same as under PROGRAM TRAPZD.

PROGRAM SIMPSON (see Table 4-3) was run for n = 10 and 100.
Both gave the same value, 0.13212 (see Table 4-4). For the
same number of subintervals, Simpson's rule gave a better approximation than the trapezoidal rule did in Example 4.2-1.

4.4 Numerical Differentiation by Central Difference Approximation

Consider the Taylor's series expansion of a function about
a point (x+h)

$$f(x+h) = f(x) + hf'(x) + \frac{h^2}{2!} f''(x) + \dots \qquad (4.4-1)$$

If we use the first two terms only and solve for $f'(x)$, we have

$$f'(x) = \frac{f(x+h) - f(x)}{h} . \qquad (4.4-2)$$

This is called the forward difference formula. Similarly, about
a point (x-h), we have

$$f'(x) = \frac{f(x) - f(x-h)}{h} . \qquad (4.4-3)$$

Eq. (4.4-3) is called the backward difference formula. Combina-
tion of Eqs. (4.4-2) and (4.4-3) yields

$$f'(x) = \frac{f(x+h) - f(x-h)}{2h} , \qquad (4.4-4)$$

which is the central difference approximation formula.

EXAMPLE 4.4-1. Numerical Differentiation by the Central
Difference Approximation Formula

The following equation which represents Gilliland's
correlation of distillation data is derived by Molokanov and
others (1972).

$$f(x) = 1 - \exp\left[\frac{(1+54.4x)(x-1)}{(11+117.2x)x^{.5}}\right]. \quad (4.4-5)$$

Evaluate f'(x) at x = 0.2 by the central difference formula.

PROGRAM DFDX

Description of Input/Output

X   -(input) the value of the independent variable

H   -(input) the increment of X

DF   -(output) the value of the derivative

PROGRAM DFDX (see Table 4-5) was run using an arbitrarily
chosen value of h = 1.0 x 10^{-5}. The value of the derivative,
DF, was -0.8569, which agrees with the analytical solution.
The computer printout is given in Table 4-6.

157

Table 4-5.   PROGRAM DFDX

```
00100      PROGRAM DFDX(INPUT,OUTPUT)
00110C
00120C     THIS PROGRAM PERFORMS NUMERICAL DIFFERENTIATION
00130C     BY THE CENTRAL DIFFERENCE APPROXIMATION FORMULA.
00140C
00150C     DEFINE FUNCTION
00160C
00170      F(X)=1.-EXP((1.+54.4*X)*(X-1.)/((11.+117.2*X)*X**.5))
00180      READ*,X,H
00190      DF=(F(X+H)-F(X-H))/(2.*H)
00200      PRINT 1,X,DF
00210    1 FORMAT(//5X,"AT X =",F6.2,5X,"DF =",F10.4)
00220      STOP
00230      END
```

Table 4-6.   An application of PROGRAM DFDX

DATA INPUT AT TIME OF EXECUTION

? .2, 1.E-5
OUTPUT

     AT X =   .20   DF =   -.8569

PROBLEMS

4-A. In a chemical process calculation we have obtained the
following equation, which relates the time required to cool
a brine solution with initial and final temperatures.

$$\theta = \int_{t_1}^{t_2} \frac{-62.4 \ dt}{0.38(t-70)^{1.25} + 0.164 \times 10^{-8}(t+460)^4 - 27.5} \ , \quad (4.A-1)$$

where θ = time (h),

t = temperature (°F), t_1 = initial temperature, t_2 = final
temperature,

How many hours are necessary to cool the solution from 150°F
to 100°F?

Answer: 14.42 h.

4-B. The error function enters into the solution of many
engineering problems involving unsteady-state conduction of
heat (Carslaw and Jaeger, 1959) and diffusion of matter (Crank,
1956). The function is defined as

$$erf(x) = \frac{2}{\sqrt{\pi}} \int_0^x e^{-z^2} \ dz. \qquad (4.B-1)$$

The integral cannot be evaluated analytically. Find erf(0.5)
and erf(1) by numerical integration.

Answer: erf(.5) = .5205,

erf(1) = .8427.

Chapter 5

Linear Interpolation

5.1 Linear Interpolation Based on Smoothed Data Points

Frequently the engineer is confronted with a collection of data relating two variables x and y in table form. If it is required to estimate the value of y for some intermediate value of x not included in the table, one may first fit the data into a polynomial function or an empirical formula, using one of the curve-fitting methods. Then the value of y may be found directly for a given value of x by evaluating the function. Interpolation by this procedure is not a problem.

If tabular data are to be used directly, some method of interpolation must be implemented. We will limit our discussions to linear interpolation because it is simple and easy to use. (Higher-order interpolation formulas, such as quadratic and cubic interpolations, are available.) The data are first plotted as points in a plane. A smooth curve is drawn passing through the points. x-y values are read from the curve at strategic locations such that the functional relation between two adjacent points may be represented by a straight line. Then the method of linear interpolation can be legitimately applied.

Linear interpolation based on smoothed data points is a convenient method, especially when the function is complicated or the nature of the function is not known. Referring to Figure 5-1, we wish to estimate the value of $y = y^*$ at $x = x^*$

by linear interpolation.

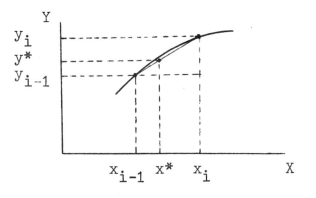

Figure 5-1. Linear interpolation

From the properties of similar triangles, we have

$$\frac{y^* - y_{i-1}}{x^* - x_{i-1}} = \frac{y_i - y_{i-1}}{x_i - x_{i-1}} \; .$$

Rearranging,

$$y^* = y_{i-1} + \left[\frac{y_i - y_{i-1}}{x_i - x_{i-1}}\right](x^* - x_{i-1}). \qquad (5.1\text{-}1)$$

In general, the method of linear interpolation using tabular data involves the following steps:

(a) The elements of the array x are arranged in ascending order,

(b) The corresponding elements of the array y are entered,

(c) The array x is searched until $x_{i-1} < x^* < x_i$,

(d) y^* is obtained by Eq. (5.1-1).

EXAMPLE 5.1-1. Linear Interpolation

Vapor-liquid equilibrium (VLE) relations are functions of temperature, pressure, and composition. Thermodynamically they are correlated in terms of fugacity coefficients and activity coefficients. The functional relations are complicated. In a computer calculation of a distillation problem, experimental VLE data could be fitted into an equation. This would represent a considerable amount of work. Or, the experimental VLE data could be used in tabular form in conjunction with a suitable interpolation formula. Owing to the complex nature of the functional relation and the fact that experimental data are subject to errors, there is no way to tell whether or not an interpolation formula will give a satisfactory result, making this approach undesirable. Thus we choose to use the simple linear interpolation based on smoothed data.

The following is a table of smoothed VLE data.

x	0	.01	.02	.03	.05	.07	.08	.10	.12	.15
y	0	.10	.17	.23	.31	.38	.40	.438	.47	.50

.17	.19	.21	.33	.40	.43	.48	.60	.64
.517	.53	.54	.583	.61	.62	.64	.70	.72

.70	.75	.80	.84	.894
.755	.785	.82	.848	.894

Write a computer program which estimates the value of y for an intermediate value of x by linear interpolation. Run the program to estimate y* at x* = .151.

Table 5-1. PROGRAM INTP1

```
00100      PROGRAM INTP1(INPUT,OUTPUT)
00110      DIMENSION X(30),Y(30)
00120      DATA X/0., .01, .02, .03, .05, .07, .08, .1, .12, .15,
00130+     .17, .19, .21, .33, .40, .43, .48, .60, .64, .70, .75,
00140+     .80, .84, .894/,
00150+     Y/0., .1, .17, .23, .31, .38, .4, .438, .47, .50, .517,
00160+     .53, .54, .583, .61, .62, .64, .7, .72, .755, .785,
00170+     .82, .848, .894/
00180      READ*,NDP,XSTAR
00190      PRINT 5,(X(I),Y(I),I=1,NDP)
00200    5 FORMAT(//6X,"X(I)",6X,"Y(I)"/(2F10.4))
00210      CALL LINT(X,Y,XSTAR,YSTAR,NDP)
00220      PRINT 10,XSTAR,YSTAR
00230   10 FORMAT(//5X,"RESULT OF INTERPOLATION"
00240+     //10X,"WHEN XSTAR =",F10.5,5X,"YSTAR =",F10.5)
00250      STOP
00260      END




00320      SUBROUTINE LINT(X,Y,XSTAR,YSTAR,N)
00330      DIMENSION X(1),Y(1)
00340      DO 10 I=1,N
00350      IF(XSTAR.LT.X(I)) GO TO 20
00360   10 CONTINUE
00370   20 YSTAR=Y(I-1)+(XSTAR-X(I-1))*(Y(I)-Y(I-1))/(X(I)-X(I-1))
00380      RETURN
00390      END
```

163

Table 5-2. An application of PROGRAM INTP1

DATA INPUT AT TIME OF EXECUTION

? 24, .151

OUTPUT

X(I)	Y(I)
0.0000	0.0000
.0100	.1000
.0200	.1700
.0300	.2300
.0500	.3100
.0700	.3800
.0800	.4000
.1000	.4380
.1200	.4700
.1500	.5000
.1700	.5170
.1900	.5300
.2100	.5400
.3300	.5830
.4000	.6100
.4300	.6200
.4800	.6400
.6000	.7000
.6400	.7200
.7000	.7550
.7500	.7850
.8000	.8200
.8400	.8480
.8940	.8940

RESULT OF INTERPOLATION

WHEN XSTAR =   .15100   YSTAR =   .50085

PROGRAM INTP1

Description of Input/Output

X   -(input) one-dimensional array containing the x-values,
           which are arranged in ascending order

Y   -(input) one-dimensional array containing the corre-
           sponding y-values

           The x-y values are entered under the DATA statement.

NDP   -(input) the number of data points

XSTAR   -(input) a given value of x

YSTAR   -(output) the y-value obtained by linear interpolation

        PROGRAM INTP1 (see Table 5-1) was run. It called
SUBROUTINE LINT to perform the search and the linear interpolation. The computer printout (see Table 5-2) gave the echo
print of the VLE data as well as the interpolated value of y.
At x* = .151, y* = .50085.

5.2 Two-Dimensional Linear Interpolation

        Suppose we have a function involving three variables,
z = f(x, y), and suppose the values of the function are
tabulated. It is required to find some intermediate value
of z within the range of the table. A two-dimensional interpolation is necessary. We can interpolate first by columns,
then by rows, or vice versa. In either case the method
involves three linear interpolations, which are best illustrated
by an example.

EXAMPLE 5.2-1.   Two-Dimensional Linear Interpolation

The specific gravities of aqueous NaOH solutions as a function of temperature and concentration are given in the following table:

Specific Gravities of NaOH Solutions
at Various Temperatures and Concentrations

Percent NaOH	Temperature, Deg. C					
	0	10	30	40	50	70
2	1.024	1.023	1.018	1.014	1.010	0.999
4	1.048	1.046	1.039	1.035	1.031	1.020
6	1.071	1.068	1.061	1.056	1.052	1.041
8	1.094	1.091	1.083	1.078	1.073	1.062
10	1.117	1.113	1.104	1.100	1.094	1.083

Estimate the specific gravity of a NaOH solution with a concentration of 5.5% NaOH at a temperature of 45°C.

We will perform linear interpolation by columns first, followed by linear interpolation by rows.

Let

i = column index,

j = row index,

x_i = tabulated values of temperature,

y_j = tabulated values of NaOH concentration,

$z_{j,i}$ = tabulated values of specific gravity,

T = the specified temperature,

C = the specified concentration of NaOH,

SG = the desired specific gravity.

We scan the table to find the column index and the row index, such that

$$x_{i-1} < T < x_i$$

and
$$y_{j-1} < C < y_j.$$

Interpolating between columns i-1 and i, we obtain two intermediate specific gravity values: S1, the value on row j-1, and S2, the value on row j.

$$S1 = z_{j-1,i-1} + \left[\frac{T - x_{i-1}}{x_i - x_{i-1}}\right](z_{j-1,i} - z_{j-1,i-1}) \qquad (5.2\text{-}1)$$

$$S2 = z_{j,i-1} + \left[\frac{T - x_{i-1}}{x_i - x_{i-1}}\right](z_{j,i} - z_{j,i-1}) \qquad (5.2\text{-}2)$$

At this point the temperature is T and the concentrations of NaOH are y_{j-1} and y_j, respectively. Now we interpolate between rows j-1 and j to obtain the desired specific gravity at temperature T and concentration C.

$$SG = S1 + \left[\frac{C - y_{j-1}}{y_j - y_{j-1}}\right](S2 - S1) \qquad (5.2\text{-}3)$$

PROGRAM INTP2D

Description of Input/Output

X   -(input) one-dimensional array containing the values
           of temperature

Y   -(input) one-dimensional array containing the values
     of NaOH concentration

Z   -(input) two-dimensional array containing the values
     of specific gravity*

M   -(input) the number of columns in the table

N   -(input) the number of rows in the table

T   -(input) the temperature for which the specific gravity
     is desired

C   -(input) the concentration of NaOH for which the specific
     gravity is desired

SG   -(output) the desired specific gravity

PROGRAM INTP2D (see Table 5-3) was run to solve Example 5.2-1. For $T = 45.0^{\circ}C$ and $C = 5.5\%$ NaOH, SG, the value of the specific gravity, was computed to be 1.0488 (see Table 5-4). The computer printout also reproduced the table of specific gravities for us to verify that the data had been entered properly. The interpolation problem was solved by columns

---

*The tabulated X, Y, and Z are entered under the DATA statement. The order in which a two-dimensional array is stored in memory is important. The computer stores the values of specific gravity in the following order:

Z(1,1), Z(2,1), Z(3,1), Z(4,1), Z(5,1), Z(1,2), Z(2,2), Z(3,2), Z(4,2), Z(5,2), ...

Therefore the table is read by columns.

first, then by rows. The order of interpolation was immaterial. The same result would have been obtained if we had interpolated first by rows, then by columns.

Table 5-3.   PROGRAM INTP2D

```
00100          PROGRAM INTP2D(INPUT,OUTPUT)
00110C         FUNCTION Z IS A TWO-DIMENSIONAL FUNCTION VERSUS X AND Y.
00120C         FOR GIVEN VALUES X=T AND Y=C, THIS PROGRAM FINDS THE
00130C         VALUE Z=SG BY TWO-DIMENSIONAL LINEAR INTERPOLATION.
00140C         X(I) AND Y(I) ARE ARRANGED IN ASCENDING ORDER.
00150C
00160          DIMENSION X(6),Y(5),Z(5,6)
00170          DATA X/0., 10., 30., 40., 50., 70./,
00180+         Y/2., 4., 6., 8., 10./,
00190+         Z/1.024, 1.048, 1.071, 1.094, 1.117,
00200+            1.023, 1.046, 1.068, 1.091, 1.113,
00210+            1.018, 1.039, 1.061, 1.083, 1.104,
00220+            1.014, 1.035, 1.056, 1.078, 1.100,
00230+            1.010, 1.031, 1.052, 1.073, 1.094,
00240+            0.999, 1.020, 1.041, 1.062, 1.083/
00250          READ*,M,N,T,C
00260C
00270C         PERFORM LINEAR INTERPOLATION, FIRST BY COLUMNS,
00280C         THEN BY ROWS.
00290C
00300          DO 10 I=1,M
00310          IF(T.LT.X(I)) GO TO 20
00320       10 CONTINUE
00330       20 DO 30 J=1,N
00340          IF(C.LT.Y(J)) GO TO 40
00350       30 CONTINUE
00360       40 S1=Z(J-1,I-1)+(T-X(I-1))/(X(I)-X(I-1))*
00370+         (Z(J-1,I)-Z(J-1,I-1))
00380          S2=Z(J,I-1)+(T-X(I-1))/(X(I)-X(I-1))*(Z(J,I)-Z(J,I-1))
00390          SG=S1+(C-Y(J-1))/(Y(J)-Y(J-1))*(S2-S1)
00400          PRINT 100,((Z(J,I),I=1,M),J=1,N)
00410      100 FORMAT(//16X,"SPECIFIC GRAVITIES OF NAOH SOLUTIONS"/
00420+         22X,"AT VARIOUS TEMPERATURES"//25X,"TEMPERATURE, DEG C"/
00425+         21X,"0",6X,"10",6X,"30",6X,"40",6X,"50",6X,"70"/
00430+         8X,"PERCENT"/10X,"NAOH"/13X,"2",6F8.3/13X,"4",6F8.3/
00450+         13X,"6",6F8.3/13X,"8",6F8.3/12X,"10",6F8.3)
00460          PRINT 50,T,C,SG
00470       50 FORMAT(//5X,"WHEN T =",F8.3,10X,"C =",F8.3/
00480+         5X,"SPECIFIC GRAVITY =",F8.4)
00490          STOP
00500          END
```

Table 5-4. An application of PROGRAM INTP2D

DATA INPUT AT TIME OF EXECUTION

? 6, 5, 45., 5.5

OUTPUT

SPECIFIC GRAVITIES OF NAOH SOLUTIONS
AT VARIOUS TEMPERATURES

	TEMPERATURE, DEG C					
	0	10	30	40	50	70
PERCENT NAOH						
2	1.024	1.023	1.018	1.014	1.010	.999
4	1.048	1.046	1.039	1.035	1.031	1.020
6	1.071	1.068	1.061	1.056	1.052	1.041
8	1.094	1.091	1.083	1.078	1.073	1.062
10	1.117	1.113	1.104	1.100	1.094	1.083

WHEN T = 45.000   C =   5.500
SPECIFIC GRAVITY =   1.0488

PROBLEMS

5-A. Show that Eqs. (5.2-1), (5.2-2), and (5.2-3) can be combined into a single equation by eliminating S1 and S2. The result is

$$SG = (1-A)(1-B)z_{j-1,i-1} + A(1-B)z_{j-1,i}$$

$$+ B(1-A)z_{j,i-1} + ABz_{j,i}, \qquad (5.A-1)$$

where $A = \dfrac{T - x_{i-1}}{x_i - x_{i-1}}$ and $B = \dfrac{C - y_{j-1}}{y_j - y_{j-1}}$.

5-B. In Example 5.2-1 we performed linear interpolation by columns first, followed by linear interpolation by rows. It was mentioned in Section 5.2 without proof that the order of interpolation was immaterial. Rework Example 5.2-1, but interpolate by rows first, then by columns. Show that the three linear interpolation steps can be combined into a single one and that the final result is the same as Eq. (5.A-1).

Chapter 6

Nonlinear Simultaneous Equations

6.1 The Newton-Raphson Method

Our problem is to find the values of x and y such that

$$f_1(x, y) = 0, \left.\right\} \qquad (6.1\text{-}1)$$
$$f_2(x, y) = 0.$$

We may use the Newton-Raphson iteration method, a method that requires initial guesses of the solution values (x_n, y_n) to get started. Expanding the functions f_1 and f_2 in Taylor series about x_n and y_n, we have

$$f_1(x_{n+1}, y_{n+1}) = f_1(x_n, y_n) + (x_{n+1} - x_n)\frac{\partial f_1}{\partial x} + (y_{n+1} - y_n)\frac{\partial f_1}{\partial y} + \ldots = 0, \left.\right\}$$
$$f_2(x_{n+1}, y_{n+1}) = f_2(x_n, y_n) + (x_{n+1} - x_n)\frac{\partial f_2}{\partial x} + (y_{n+1} - y_n)\frac{\partial f_2}{\partial y} + \ldots = 0. \qquad (6.1\text{-}2)$$

where

$$\left\{ \begin{array}{l} x_{n+1} = x_n + \Delta x, \\ y_{n+1} = y_n + \Delta y. \end{array} \right.$$

If we truncate the Taylor series to linear terms only, we have

$$-f_1(x_n, y_n) \approx (\Delta x)\frac{\partial f_1}{\partial x} + (\Delta y)\frac{\partial f_1}{\partial y}, \left.\right\}$$
$$-f_2(x_n, y_n) \approx (\Delta x)\frac{\partial f_2}{\partial x} + (\Delta y)\frac{\partial f_2}{\partial y}. \qquad (6.1\text{-}3)$$

Eq. (6.1-3) is a set of linear equations in Δx and Δy. These differences can be evaluated as follows:

$$\Delta x = \dfrac{\begin{vmatrix} -f_1 & \dfrac{\partial f_1}{\partial y} \\[2ex] -f_2 & \dfrac{\partial f_2}{\partial y} \end{vmatrix}}{\begin{vmatrix} \dfrac{\partial f_1}{\partial x} & \dfrac{\partial f_1}{\partial y} \\[2ex] \dfrac{\partial f_2}{\partial x} & \dfrac{\partial f_2}{\partial y} \end{vmatrix}}, \qquad \Delta y = \dfrac{\begin{vmatrix} \dfrac{\partial f_1}{\partial x} & -f_1 \\[2ex] \dfrac{\partial f_2}{\partial x} & -f_2 \end{vmatrix}}{\begin{vmatrix} \dfrac{\partial f_1}{\partial x} & \dfrac{\partial f_1}{\partial y} \\[2ex] \dfrac{\partial f_2}{\partial x} & \dfrac{\partial f_2}{\partial y} \end{vmatrix}}. \qquad (6.1\text{-}4)$$

Functions f_1 and f_2 and the partial derivatives are all evaluated at x_n and y_n. In general, the Newton-Raphson method updates the (n+1)th approximation from the nth approximation through the relations

$$\left. \begin{aligned} x_{n+1} &= x_n + \Delta x, \\ y_{n+1} &= y_n + \Delta y. \end{aligned} \right\} \qquad (6.1\text{-}5)$$

The iteration continues until the values of x and y stabilize. However, there is no guarantee that the method will always converge. The extension of these techniques to systems of three or more equations is straightforward.

EXAMPLE 6.1-1. Three-Stage Crosscurrent Extraction

In the three-stage crosscurrent extraction of Example 1.4-2, the feed rate was 300 L/h, and the composition x_F was 0.10. The solute concentration in the raffinate, x_3, was reduced to 0.05. Now we intend to find the minimum amount of solvent necessary to achieve the required separation. (The amount of solvent added to each stage does not have to be the same.)

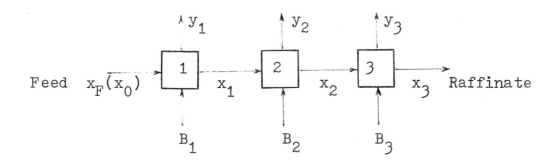

Figure 6-1. A 3-stage crosscurrent extractor

Let

A = flow rate of the feed stream (300 L/h),

B = flow rate of the solvent stream: B_1, B_2, and B_3 are the flow rates of solvents to stages 1, 2, and 3, respectively, B_T is the sum of B_1, B_2, and B_3,

x = solute concentration in the raffinate phase, x_F is the feed composition (0.01), x_3 is the raffinate composition (0.05),

y = solute concentration in the extract phase, y_s is the composition of the solvent (y_s = 0 for pure solvent).

The extractor has three ideal stages. The streams leaving a stage are in equilibrium. The equilibrium relation is represented by

$$y = \alpha x^\beta ,$$

where

$$\alpha = 2.5 \quad \text{and} \quad \beta = 1.194.$$

The two liquid streams are immiscible.

A material balance of the solute around stage 1 yields

$$Ax_F + B_1 y_S = Ax_1 + B_1 y_1. \tag{6.1-6}$$

From the equilibrium relation we have

$$y_1 = \alpha x_1^\beta. \tag{6.1-7}$$

Eliminating y_1 from Eqs. (6.1-6) and (6.1-7) and solving for B_1, we have

$$B_1 = \frac{A(x_F - x_1)}{\alpha x_1^\beta}. \tag{6.1-8}$$

Similarly, material balances around stages 2 and 3 give

$$B_2 = \frac{A(x_1 - x_2)}{\alpha x_2^\beta}, \tag{6.1-9}$$

$$B_3 = \frac{A(x_2 - x_3)}{\alpha x_3^\beta}. \tag{6.1-10}$$

$$B_T = B_1 + B_2 + B_3 = \frac{A}{\alpha}\left[\frac{x_F - x_1}{x_1^\beta} + \frac{x_1 - x_2}{x_2^\beta} + \frac{x_2 - x_3}{x_3^\beta}\right]. \tag{6.1-11}$$

Since the total amount of solvent is to be a minimum, the partial derivatives of B_T with respect to x_1 and x_2 must be zero.

$$\frac{\partial B_T}{\partial x_1} = 0 = -\frac{1}{x_1^\beta} - \frac{\beta(x_F - x_1)}{x_1^{\beta+1}} + \frac{1}{x_2^\beta} = \phi_1,$$

$$\frac{\partial B_T}{\partial x_2} = 0 = -\frac{1}{x_2^\beta} - \frac{\beta(x_1 - x_2)}{x_2^{\beta+1}} + \frac{1}{x_3^\beta} = \phi_2.$$

Simplifying,

$$\phi_1 = x_1^{\beta+1} + (\beta-1)x_1 x_2^\beta - \beta\, x_F x_2^\beta = 0, \qquad (6.1-12)$$

$$\phi_2 = x_2^{\beta+1} + (\beta-1)x_2 x_3^\beta - \beta\, x_1 x_3^\beta = 0. \qquad (6.1-13)$$

The problem now reduces to the solution of Eqs. (6.1-12) and (6.1-13) simultaneously for x_1 and x_2. The results can then be substituted into Eqs. (6.1-8) through (6.1-11) to obtain the amount of solvent required. We will use the Newton-Raphson method. The four partial derivatives are

$$\frac{\partial \phi_1}{\partial x_1} = (\beta+1)x_1^\beta + (\beta-1)x_2^\beta, \qquad (6.1-14)$$

$$\frac{\partial \phi_1}{\partial x_2} = \beta\left[(\beta-1)x_1 - \beta\, x_F\right]x_2^{\beta-1}, \qquad (6.1-15)$$

$$\frac{\partial \phi_2}{\partial x_1} = -\beta\, x_3^\beta, \qquad (6.1-16)$$

$$\frac{\partial \phi_2}{\partial x_2} = (\beta+1)x_2^\beta + (\beta-1)x_3^\beta. \qquad (6.1-17)$$

We need initial guesses of x_1 and x_2 to start the Newton-Raphson iteration. It is obvious that

$$x_F > x_1 > x_2 > x_3.$$

Thus we may use $x_1 = 0.08$ and $x_2 = 0.06$ to start the iteration. We continue until the values stabilize.

PROGRAM EXTN2A

Description of Input/Output

A   -(input) the flow rate of the feed stream

XF   -(input) the composition of the feed

X(3)   -(input) the composition of the final raffinate

X(1)   -(input) the initially guessed value of X(1)

X(2)   -(input) the initially guessed value of X(2)

EPS   -(input) the tolerance limit for convergence

B   -(output) one-dimensional array containing the converged
         values of solvent to each stage

BT   -(output) total amount of solvent

X   -(output) one-dimensional array containing the converged
         values of compositions in the raffinate phase

Y   -(output) one-dimensional array containing the converged
         values of compositions in the extract phase

PROGRAM EXTN2A (see Table 6-1) was run to solve the three-stage crosscurrent extraction problem of Example 6.1-1, using the tolerance limit, EPS = 1 x 10^{-7}, for both ϕ_1 and ϕ_2. After two iterations, the following results (see Table 6-2) were obtained.

Stage no.	x_i	y_i	B_i
1	.07899	.12068	52.23
2	.06270	.09159	53.36
3	.05000	.06991	54.50

Total solvent = 160.08 (rounded to the second decimal)

178

Table 6-1.   PROGRAM EXTN2A

```
00100          PROGRAM EXTN2A(INPUT,OUTPUT)
00110C
00120C         THIS PROGRAM CALCULATES THE MINIMUM SOLVENT REQUIRED
00130C         FOR A SPECIFIED SEPARATION IN A THREE-STAGE CROSS-
00140C         CURRENT EXTRACTOR.   THE NEWTON-RAPHSON METHOD IS USED
00150C         TO SOLVE THE SET OF NONLINEAR EQUATIONS.
00160C
00170          DIMENSION X(3),Y(3),B(3),PHI(2),DELX(2),DERIV(2,2)
00180C
00190C         DATA INPUT
00200C
00210          READ*,A,XF,X(3)
00220C
00230C         INITIAL GUESS OF X(1) AND X(2) TO GET STARTED
00240C
00250          READ*,X(1),X(2),EPS
00260C
00270C         EVALUATE THE TWO FUNCTIONS
00280C
00290          ITER=1
00300          PRINT 5
00310        5 FORMAT(//" ITER",5X,"X(1)",6X,"X(2)",6X,"X(3)"/)
00320       10 PHI(1)=X(1)**2.194+.194*X(1)*X(2)**1.194
00330+          -1.194*XF*X(2)**1.194
00340          PHI(2)=X(2)**2.194+.194*X(2)*X(3)**1.194
00350+          -1.194*X(1)*X(3)**1.194
00360          IF(ABS(PHI(1)).LT.EPS.AND.ABS(PHI(2)).LT.EPS) GO TO 30
00370C
00380C         THE FOUR PARTIAL DERIVATIVES
00390C
00400          DERIV(1,1)=2.194*X(1)**1.194+.194*X(2)**1.194
00410          DERIV(1,2)=1.194*(.194*X(1)-1.194*XF)*X(2)**.194
00420          DERIV(2,1)=-1.194*X(3)**1.194
00430          DERIV(2,2)=2.194*X(2)**1.194+.194*X(3)**1.194
00440          D=DERIV(1,1)*DERIV(2,2)-DERIV(1,2)*DERIV(2,1)
00450          DELX(1)=(PHI(2)*DERIV(1,2)-PHI(1)*DERIV(2,2))/D
00460          DELX(2)=(PHI(1)*DERIV(2,1)-PHI(2)*DERIV(1,1))/D
00470          DO 20 I=1,2
00480       20 X(I)=X(I)+DELX(I)
00490          PRINT 25,ITER,(X(I),I=1,3)
00500       25 FORMAT(I5,3F10.5)
00510          ITER=ITER+1
00520          GO TO 10
00530C
00540C         CONVERGENCE ACHIEVED, PRINTOUT ANSWERS
00550C
00560       30 DO 40 I=1,3
00570       40 Y(I)=2.5*X(I)**1.194
00580          B(1)=A*(XF-X(1))/Y(1)
00590          B(2)=A*(X(1)-X(2))/Y(2)
00600          B(3)=A*(X(2)-X(3))/Y(3)
00610          BT=B(1)+B(2)+B(3)
00620          PRINT 50
00630       50 FORMAT(//"   CONVERGENCE ACHIEVED"/)
00640          PRINT 60,(X(I),I=1,3)
00650       60 FORMAT(/" X(I)'S",3F10.5)
```

```
00660        PRINT 70,(Y(I),I=1,3)
00670     70 FORMAT(/" Y(I)'S",3F10.5)
00680        PRINT 80,(B(I),I=1,3)
00690     80 FORMAT(/" B(I)'S",F7.2,2F10.2)
00700        PRINT 90,BT
00710     90 FORMAT(/" MINIMUM SOLVENT REQUIREMENT =",F10.2,
00720+       " L/HR")
00730        STOP
00740        END
```

Table 6-2. An application of PROGRAM EXTN2A

DATA INPUT AT TIME OF EXECUTION

```
? 300., .1, .05
? .08, .06, 1.E-7
OUTPUT

  ITER     X(1)      X(2)      X(3)

    1     .07904    .06279    .05000
    2     .07899    .06270    .05000


     CONVERGENCE ACHIEVED


  X(I)'S    .07899     .06270     .05000

  Y(I)'S    .12068     .09159     .06991

  B(I)'S  52.23      53.36      54.50

MINIMUM SOLVENT REQUIREMENT =    160.08 L/HR
```

The total amount of solvent required was practically the same as that in Example 1.4-2, which specified that equal amounts of solvent were to be used in the three stages.

EXAMPLE 6.1-2. Adiabatic Flash

In Example 1.3-4, the flash process was carried out at specified temperature and pressure. Another type of problem is adiabatic flash, which is to determine the temperature of the flash, the fraction vaporized, and the corresponding vapor and liquid compositions when the pressure of the flash and the enthalpy of the feed are specified.

Consider the adiabatic flash of a feed with the following composition:

Component	Mole fraction
1	.40
2	.30
3	.30

The pressure is 1 atm. The enthalpy of the feed mixture is 36927 Btu/lb-mole. Under the given conditions the equilibrium relation and the liquid and vapor enthalpies can be represented by the following equations:

$$\ln K = A_K + B_K T + C_K T^2, \qquad (6.1\text{-}18)$$

$$H_L = A_L + B_L T + C_L T^2, \qquad (6.1\text{-}19)$$

$$H_V = A_V + B_V T + C_V T^2, \qquad (6.1\text{-}20)$$

where K = vapor-liquid equilibrium ratio = y/x,

   T = temperature, $^{\circ}F$,

   H_L = enthalpy of a component in the liquid phase,
      Btu/lb-mole,

   H_V = enthalpy of a component in the vapor phase,
      Btu/lb-mole,

  A,B,C = constants which are characteristic of a component.

Component	A_K	B_K	C_K
1	-2.9928	.022270	-1.8669×10^{-4}
2	-5.9045	.029968	$-.27439 \times 10^{-4}$
3	-8.7205	.037367	$-.35124 \times 10^{-4}$

Component	A_L	B_L	C_L
1	$.78531 \times 10^{4}$	$.44004 \times 10^{2}$	.029633
2	$.11772 \times 10^{5}$	$.49248 \times 10^{2}$	.041793
3	$.14334 \times 10^{5}$	$.60363 \times 10^{2}$	.046374

Component	A_V	B_V	C_V
1	$.21960 \times 10^{5}$	$.37800 \times 10^{2}$	0
2	$.30356 \times 10^{5}$	$.39949 \times 10^{2}$	.023254
3	$.36859 \times 10^{5}$	$.49436 \times 10^{2}$	.032343

Find (a) the temperature of the flash,

   (b) the fraction vaporized,

   (c) the corresponding liquid and vapor compositions.

The material balances and equilibrium relations are the
same as those in Example 1.3-4. Therefore, Eqs. (1.3-18),

183

(1.3-19), (1.3-20), and (1.3-21) apply, except that in adiabatic flash the temperature is an unknown. The expression in Eq. (1.3-21) is now a function of two independent variables, T and V.

$$g_1(T,V) = \sum \frac{z_i(K_i - 1)}{1 + V(K_i - 1)} = 0. \qquad (1.3-21)$$

Eq. (1.3-21) is written for 1 mole of feed. V is the fraction vaporized. In order to solve both T and V, we need another equation, which is obtained by enthalpy balance.

$$g_2(T,V) = V \cdot ENTHV + (1-V) \cdot ENTHL - HF = 0, \qquad (6.1-21)$$

where ENTHV = enthalpy of the vapor mixture, Btu/lb-mole,

ENTHL = enthalpy of the liquid mixture, Btu/lb-mole,

HF = enthalpy of the feed mixture, Btu/lb-mole.

The two quantities, ENTHV and ENTHL in Eq. (6.1-21), are obtained from the following:

$$ENTHV = \sum H_{Vi} y_i, \qquad (6.1-22)$$

$$ENTHL = \sum H_{Li} x_i. \qquad (6.1-23)$$

H_{Vi} and H_{Li} are defined by Eqs. (6.1-20) and (6.1-19), respectively. Subscript i refers to the i-th component. x_i and y_i are given by Eqs. (1.3-18) and (1.3-19).

Now we have two equations g_1 and g_2 in two unknowns T and V. They are solved by the Newton-Raphson method.

The four partial derivatives are

$$\frac{\partial g_1}{\partial T} = \sum \frac{z_i K_i (B_{Ki} + 2C_{Ki}T)}{\left[1 + V(K_i - 1)\right]^2} \, , \qquad\qquad (6.1\text{-}24)$$

$$\frac{\partial g_1}{\partial V} = -\sum \frac{z_i (K_i - 1)^2}{\left[1 + V(K_i - 1)\right]^2} \, , \qquad\qquad (6.1\text{-}25)$$

$$\frac{\partial g_2}{\partial T} = V \frac{\partial (\text{ENTHV})}{\partial T} + (1-V) \frac{\partial (\text{ENTHL})}{\partial T}$$

$$= V\left[\sum \frac{z_i K_i (B_{Vi} + 2C_{Vi}T)}{1 + V(K_i - 1)} + \sum \frac{z_i K_i H_{Vi}(1-V)(B_{Ki} + 2C_{Ki}T)}{\left[1 + V(K_i - 1)\right]^2}\right]$$

$$+ (1-V)\left[\sum \frac{z_i (B_{Li} + 2C_{Li}T)}{1 + V(K_i - 1)} - \sum \frac{z_i K_i H_{Li}V(B_{Ki} + 2C_{Ki}T)}{\left[1 + V(K_i - 1)\right]^2}\right], \quad (6.1\text{-}26)$$

$$\frac{\partial g_2}{\partial V} = \sum \frac{z_i K_i (H_{Vi} - H_{Li})}{\left[1 + V(K_i - 1)\right]^2} \, . \qquad\qquad (6.1\text{-}27)$$

We use initially guessed values of T and V to start the Newton-Raphson method. It has been pointed out previously in Section 1.3 that the flash temperature is somewhere between the bubble-point and dew-point temperature. A temperature of 250°F is a reasonable guess. The fraction vaporized, of course, is between 0 and 1. We arbitrarily choose 0.5.

PROGRAM ADFLSH

Description of Input/Output

The parameters AK, BK, CK, AL, BL, CL, AV, BV, CV, and the feed composition Z are entered under the DATA statement.

185

AK,BK,CK - one-dimensional arrays containing parameters in the K-value equation

AL,BL,CL - one-dimensional arrays containing parameters in the liquid enthalpy equation

AV,BV,CV - one-dimensional arrays containing parameters in the vapor enthalpy equation

Z   - one-dimensional array containing the feed composition

NOC   -(input) the number of components

HF   -(input) the enthalpy of the feed mixture, Btu/lb-mole

T   -(input) initial guess of the flash temperature, ^{o}F

V   -(input) initial guess of the fraction vaporized

T   -(output) the converged value of the flash temperature

V   -(output) the converged value of the fraction vaporized

X   -(output) one-dimensional array containing the liquid compositions

Y   -(output) one-dimensional array containing the vapor compositions

ENTHL -(output) the enthalpy of the liquid mixture, Btu/lb-mole

ENTHV -(output) the enthalpy of the vapor mixture, Btu/lb-mole

PROGRAM ADFLSH (see Table 6-3) was run under the following conditions:

Initial guess of T = 250,

Initial guess of V = 0.5,

Convergence criteria -- ±0.01 for T; ±0.0001 for V.

Convergence was achieved after three iterations. The results (see Table 6-4) were

Table 6-3. PROGRAM ADFLSH

```
00100          PROGRAM ADFLSH(INPUT,OUTPUT)
00110          REAL K(10)
00120          DIMENSION AK(10),BK(10),CK(10),AL(10),BL(10),CL(10),
00130+         AV(10),BV(10),CV(10),X(10),Y(10),Z(10),HV(10),HL(10),
00140+         G(2),DG(2,2)
00150          DATA AK/-2.99279, -5.90449, -8.72046/,BK/2.227E-2,
00160+         2.9968E-2, 3.7367E-2/,CK/-1.8669E-5, -2.7439E-5,
00170+         -3.5124E-5/,AL/.78531E4, 1.17715E4, 1.43337E4/,
00180+         BL/.44004E2, .49248E2, .60363E2/,CL/.29633E-1,
00190+         .41793E-1, .46374E-1/,AV/.2196E5, .30356E5,
00200+         .36859E5/,BV/.37800E2, .39949E2, .49436E2/,
00210+         CV/0., .23254E-1, .32343E-1/,Z/.4, .3, .3/
00220C
00230C         DATA INPUT AND ECHO PRINT
00240C
00250          READ*,NOC,HF
00260C
00270C         INITIAL GUESS OF T AND V
00280C
00290          READ*,T,V
00300          PRINT 101,NOC
00310   101 FORMAT(//," THE NO. OF COMPONENTS =",I3)
00320          PRINT 102,(Z(I),I=1,NOC)
00330          G(2)=0.
00340   102 FORMAT(/," THE VALUES OF Z(I)'S ARE"/(3F10.4))
00350          PRINT 103,HF
00360   103 FORMAT(/" THE ENTHALPY OF FEED =",F10.0," BTU/LB-MOLE")
00370          PRINT 104,(AK(I),BK(I),CK(I),I=1,NOC)
00380   104 FORMAT(/" THE VALUES OF AK(I), BK(I), AND CK(I) ARE"/
00390+         (3E15.5))
00400          PRINT 105,(AL(I),BL(I),CL(I),I=1,NOC)
00410   105 FORMAT(/" THE VALUES OF AL(I), BL(I), AND CL(I) ARE"/
00420+         (3E15.5))
00430          PRINT 106,(AV(I),BV(I),CV(I),I=1,NOC)
00440   106 FORMAT(/" THE VALUES OF AV(I), BV(I), AND CV(I) ARE"/
00450+         (3E15.5))
00460          PRINT 107
00470   107 FORMAT(///5X,"ITER",6X,"T",9X,"V")
00480          ITER=1
00490C
00500C         EVALUATE FUNCTIONS G(1), G(2), AND THE FOUR PARTIAL
00510C         DERIVATIVES
00520C
00530     5 PRINT 108,ITER,T,V
00540   108 FORMAT(I9,F10.2,F10.4)
00550          G(1)=0.
00560          DG(1,1)=0.
00570          DG(1,2)=0.
00590          DG(2,2)=0.
00600          SUM1=0.
00610          SUM2=0.
00620          ENTHV=0.
00630          ENTHL=0.
00640          DO 10 I=1,NOC
00650          K(I)=EXP(AK(I)+BK(I)*T+CK(I)*T*T)
00660          S1=BK(I)+2.*CK(I)*T
```

```
00670        S2=1.+V*(K(I)-1.)
00680        S3=BV(I)+2.*CV(I)*T
00690        S4=BL(I)+2.*CL(I)*T
00700        HV(I)=AV(I)+BV(I)*T+CV(I)*T*T
00710        HL(I)=AL(I)+BL(I)*T+CL(I)*T*T
00720        G(1)=G(1)+Z(I)*(K(I)-1.)/S2
00730        DG(1,1)=DG(1,1)+Z(I)*K(I)*S1/S2**2
00740        DG(1,2)=DG(1,2)-Z(I)*(K(I)-1.)**2/S2**2
00750        DG(2,2)=DG(2,2)+(HV(I)-HL(I))*K(I)*Z(I)/S2**2
00760        ENTHV=ENTHV+HV(I)*K(I)*Z(I)/S2
00770        ENTHL=ENTHL+HL(I)*Z(I)/S2
00780        SUM1=SUM1+K(I)*Z(I)*S3/S2+K(I)*Z(I)*HV(I)*(1.-V)*S1/
00790+       S2**2
00800     10 SUM2=SUM2+Z(I)*S4/S2-K(I)*Z(I)*HL(I)*V*S1/S2**2
00810        G(2)=V*ENTHV+(1.-V)*ENTHL-HF
00820        DG(2,1)=V*SUM1+(1.-V)*SUM2
00830C
00840C       UPDATE T AND V BY NEWTON-RAPHSON METHOD
00850C
00860        D=DG(1,1)*DG(2,2)-DG(1,2)*DG(2,1)
00870        DELT=(G(2)*DG(1,2)-G(1)*DG(2,2))/D
00880        DELV=(G(1)*DG(2,1)-G(2)*DG(1,1))/D
00890        IF(ABS(DELT).LT..01.AND.ABS(DELV).LT..0001) GO TO 40
00900        T=T+DELT
00910        V=V+DELV
00920        ITER=ITER+1
00930        GO TO 5
00940C
00950C       CONVERGENCE ACHIEVED, PRINT ANSWERS
00960C
00970     40 DO 50 I=1,NOC
00980        X(I)=Z(I)/(1.+V*(K(I)-1.))
00990     50 Y(I)=K(I)*X(I)
01000        PRINT 201,T
01010    201 FORMAT(//" THE TEMPERATURE OF FLASH =",F8.2," DEG F"/)
01020        PRINT 202,V
01030    202 FORMAT(" FRACTION VAPORIZED =",F8.4/)
01040        PRINT 203,(X(I),I=1,NOC)
01050    203 FORMAT(" THE X(I)'S ARE"/(3F10.4)/)
01060        PRINT 204,(Y(I),I=1,NOC)
01070    204 FORMAT(" THE Y(I)'S ARE"/(3F10.4)/)
01080        PRINT 205, ENTHL
01090    205 FORMAT(" THE ENTHALPY OF LIQUID =",F10.0,
01100+       " BTU/LB-MOLE")
01110        PRINT 206,ENTHV
01120    206 FORMAT(" THE ENTHALPY OF VAPOR =",F11.0,
01130+       " BTU/LB-MOLE")
01140        STOP
01150        END
```

Table 6-4. An application of PROGRAM ADFLSH

DATA INPUT AT TIME OF EXECUTION

```
? 3, 36927.
? 250., .5
OUTPUT

THE NO. OF COMPONENTS =  3

THE VALUES OF Z(I)'S ARE
    .4000       .3000        .3000

THE ENTHALPY OF FEED =    36927. BTU/LB-MOLE

THE VALUES OF AK(I), BK(I), AND CK(I) ARE
   -.29928E+01        .22270E-01       -.18669E-04
   -.59045E+01        .29968E-01       -.27439E-04
   -.87205E+01        .37367E-01       -.35124E-04

THE VALUES OF AL(I), BL(I), AND CL(I) ARE
    .78531E+04        .44004E+02        .29633E-01
    .11772E+05        .49248E+02        .41793E-01
    .14334E+05        .60363E+02        .46374E-01

THE VALUES OF AV(I), BV(I), AND CV(I) ARE
    .21960E+05        .37800E+02        0.
    .30356E+05        .39949E+02        .23254E-01
    .36859E+05        .49436E+02        .32343E-01


    ITER      T          V
      1     250.00      .5000
      2     268.54      .7398
      3     267.15      .7363


THE TEMPERATURE OF FLASH =  267.15 DEG F

FRACTION VAPORIZED =    .7363

THE X(I)'S ARE
    .1000      .2695       .6306

THE Y(I)'S ARE
    .5074      .3109       .1816

THE ENTHALPY OF LIQUID =    30987. BTU/LB-MOLE
THE ENTHALPY OF VAPOR =     39054. BTU/LB-MOLE
```

189

Temperature of the flash = 267.15°F,

Fraction vaporized = .7363,

The equilibrium liquid and vapor compositions are:

Component	x_i	y_i
1	.1000	.5074
2	.2695	.3109
3	.6306	.1816

In PROGRAM ADFLSH the four partial derivatives are evaluated analytically by Eqs. (6.1-24) through (6.1-27). They can also be obtained by the finite difference method described in Chapter 4.

$$\frac{\partial g_1}{\partial T} = \frac{g_1(T+h_1, V) - g_1(T, V)}{h_1}, \qquad (6.1-28)$$

$$\frac{\partial g_1}{\partial V} = \frac{g_1(T, V+h_2) - g_1(T, V)}{h_2}, \qquad (6.1-29)$$

$$\frac{\partial g_2}{\partial T} = \frac{g_2(T+h_1, V) - g_2(T, V)}{h_1}, \qquad (6.1-30)$$

$$\frac{\partial g_2}{\partial V} = \frac{g_2(T, V+h_2) - g_2(T, V)}{h_2}, \qquad (6.1-31)$$

where h_1 and h_2 are small increments of T and V, respectively.

PROGRAM ADFLSH2 (see Table 6-5) was prepared with a numerical method to evaluate the partial derivatives. A subprogram FUNCTION FUNC was included to evaluate functions g_1, g_2, and the four partial derivatives. The increments $h_1 = 10^{-3}$ and $h_2 = 10^{-6}$ were found to be satisfactory. In order to make the values of AK, BK, CK, ... available to the subroutine as well as to the main program, we put these variables under the COMMON statement. We also chose to initialize them in a DATA statement. The system requires (a) that the variables be assigned to a labeled COMMON, and (b) that they be initialized in a BLOCK DATA subprogram.

PROGRAM ADFLSH2

Description of Input/Output

Same as in PROGRAM ADFLSH. Notice the variables initialized in a BLOCK DATA subprogram. They appear in a labeled COMMON (block A).

PROGRAM ADFLSH2 (see Table 6-5) was run with the same input as PROGRAM ADFLSH. Identical results (see Table 6-6) were obtained. Numerical differentiation was employed in this example, and it worked well.

Table 6-5. PROGRAM ADFLSH2

```
00100        PROGRAM ADFLSH2 (INPUT,OUTPUT)
00110        REAL K(10)
00120        COMMON/A/AK(10),BK(10),CK(10),AL(10),BL(10),CL(10),
00130+       AV(10),BV(10),CV(10),Z(10)
00140        COMMON/B/K,HV(10),HL(10),ENTHV,ENTHL,HF,NOC
00150        DIMENSION G(2),DG(2,2),X(10),Y(10)
00160C
00170C       DATA INPUT AND ECHO PRINT
00180C
00190        READ*,NOC,HF
00200C
00210C       INITIAL GUESS OF T AND V
00220C
00230        READ*,T,V
00240        PRINT 101,NOC
00250   101 FORMAT(//," THE NO. OF COMPONENTS =",I3)
00260        PRINT 102,(Z(I),I=1,NOC)
00270   102 FORMAT(/," THE VALUES OF Z(I)'S ARE"/(3F10.4))
00280        PRINT 103,HF
00290   103 FORMAT(/" THE ENTHALPY OF FEED =",F10.0," BTU/LB-MOLE")
00300        PRINT 104,(AK(I),BK(I),CK(I),I=1,NOC)
00310   104 FORMAT(/" THE VALUES OF AK(I), BK(I), AND CK(I) ARE"/
00320+       (3E15.5))
00330        PRINT 105,(AL(I),BL(I),CL(I),I=1,NOC)
00340   105 FORMAT(/" THE VALUES OF AL(I), BL(I), AND CL(I) ARE"/
00350+       (3E15.5))
00360        PRINT 106,(AV(I),BV(I),CV(I),I=1,NOC)
00370   106 FORMAT(/" THE VALUES OF AV(I), BV(I), AND CV(I) ARE"/
00380+       (3E15.5))
00390        PRINT 107
00400   107 FORMAT(///5X,"ITER",6X,"T",9X,"V")
00410        ITER=1
00420C
00430C       EVALUATE THE FUNCTIONS G(1) AND G(2)
00440C
00450     5 PRINT 108,ITER,T,V
00460   108 FORMAT(I9,F10.2,F10.4)
00470        DO 10 I=1,2
00480    10 G(I)=FUNC(I,T,V)
00490C
00500C       EVALUATE THE FOUR PARTIAL DERIVATIVES BY FINITE
00510C       DIFFERENCE METHOD
00520C
00530        H1=.001
00540        H2=.000001
00550        DO 20 I=1,2
00560        DG(I,1)=(FUNC(I,T+H1,V)-G(I))/H1
00570    20 DG(I,2)=(FUNC(I,T,V+H2)-G(I))/H2
00580C
00590C       UPDATE T AND V BY NEWTON-RAPHSON METHOD
00600C
00610        D=DG(1,1)*DG(2,2)-DG(1,2)*DG(2,1)
00620        DELT=(G(2)*DG(1,2)-G(1)*DG(2,2))/D
00630        DELV=(G(1)*DG(2,1)-G(2)*DG(1,1))/D
00640        IF(ABS(DELT).LT..01.AND.ABS(DELV).LT..0001) GO TO 40
```

```
00650      T=T+DELT
00660      V=V+DELV
00670      ITER=ITER+1
00680      GO TO 5
00690C
00700C     CONVERGENCE ACHIEVED, PRINT ANSWERS
00710C
00720   40 DO 50 I=1,NOC
00730      X(I)=Z(I)/(1.+V*(K(I)-1.))
00740   50 Y(I)=K(I)*X(I)
00750      PRINT 201,T
00760  201 FORMAT(//" THE TEMPERATURE OF FLASH =",F8.2," DEG F"/)
00770      PRINT 202,V
00780  202 FORMAT(" FRACTION VAPORIZED =",F8.4/)
00790      PRINT 203,(X(I),I=1,NOC)
00800  203 FORMAT(" THE X(I)'S ARE"/(3F10.4)/)
00810      PRINT 204,(Y(I),I=1,NOC)
00820  204 FORMAT(" THE Y(I)'S ARE"/(3F10.4)/)
00830      PRINT 205, ENTHL
00840  205 FORMAT(" THE ENTHALPY OF LIQUID =",F10.0,
00850+     " BTU/LB-MOLE")
00860      PRINT 206,ENTHV
00870  206 FORMAT(" THE ENTHALPY OF VAPOR =",F11.0,
00880+     " BTU/LB-MOLE")
00890      STOP
00900      END



00940      FUNCTION FUNC(M,T,V)
00950      REAL K(10)
00960      COMMON/A/AK(10),BK(10),CK(10),AL(10),BL(10),CL(10),
00970+     AV(10),BV(10),CV(10),Z(10)
00980      COMMON/B/K,HV(10),HL(10),ENTHV,ENTHL,HF,NOC
00990      GO TO (1,2)M
01000    1 FUNC=0.
01010      DO 10 I=1,NOC
01020      K(I)=EXP(AK(I)+BK(I)*T+CK(I)*T*T)
01030   10 FUNC=FUNC+Z(I)*(K(I)-1.)/(1.+V*(K(I)-1.))
01040      RETURN
01050    2 DO 20 I=1,NOC
01060      K(I)=EXP(AK(I)+BK(I)*T+CK(I)*T*T)
01070      HV(I)=AV(I)+BV(I)*T+CV(I)*T*T
01080   20 HL(I)=AL(I)+BL(I)*T+CL(I)*T*T
01090      ENTHV=0.
01100      ENTHL=0.
01110      DO 30 I=1,NOC
01120      S=1.+V*(K(I)-1.)
01130      ENTHV=ENTHV+HV(I)*K(I)*Z(I)/S
01140   30 ENTHL=ENTHL+HL(I)*Z(I)/S
01150      FUNC=V*ENTHV+(1.-V)*ENTHL-HF
01160      RETURN
01170      END
```

```
01180      BLOCK DATA
01190      REAL K(10)
01200      COMMON/A/AK(10),BK(10),CK(10),AL(10),BL(10),CL(10),
01210+     AV(10),BV(10),CV(10),Z(10)
01220      COMMON/B/K,HV(10),HL(10),ENTHV,ENTHL,HF,NOC
01230      DATA AK/-2.99279, -5.90449, -8.72046/,BK/2.227E-2,
01240+     2.9968E-2, 3.7367E-2/,CK/-1.8669E-5, -2.7439E-5,
01250+     -3.5124E-5/,AL/.78531E4,1.17715E4, 1.43337E4/,
01260+     BL/.44004E2, .49248E2, .60363E2/,CL/.29633E-1,
01270+     .41793E-1, .46374E-1/,AV/.2196E5, .30356E5,
01280+     .36859E5/,BV/.37800E2, .39949E2, .49436E2/,
01290+     CV/0., .23254E-1, .32343E-1/,Z/.4, .3, .3/
01300      END
```

Table 6-6. An application of PROGRAM ADFLSH2

DATA INPUT AT TIME OF EXECUTION

? 3, 36927.
? 250., .5

OUTPUT

 THE NO. OF COMPONENTS =   3

 THE VALUES OF Z(I)'S ARE
     .4000   .3000   .3000

 THE ENTHALPY OF FEED =   36927. BTU/LB-MOLE

 THE VALUES OF AK(I), BK(I), AND CK(I) ARE
     -.29928E+01   .22270E-01   -.18669E-04
     -.59045E+01   .29968E-01   -.27439E-04
     -.87205E+01   .37367E-01   -.35124E-04

 THE VALUES OF AL(I), BL(I), AND CL(I) ARE
      .78531E+04   .44004E+02   .29633E-01
      .11772E+05   .49248E+02   .41793E-01
      .14334E+05   .60363E+02   .46374E-01

 THE VALUES OF AV(I), BV(I), AND CV(I) ARE
      .21960E+05   .37800E+02   0.
      .30356E+05   .39949E+02   .23254E-01
      .36859E+05   .49436E+02   .32343E-01

     ITER   T   V
       1   250.00   .5000
       2   268.54   .7398
       3   267.15   .7363

 THE TEMPERATURE OF FLASH = 267.15 DEG F

 FRACTION VAPORIZED =   .7363

 THE X(I)'S ARE
     .1000   .2695   .6306

 THE Y(I)'S ARE
     .5074   .3109   .1816

 THE ENTHALPY OF LIQUID =   30987. BTU/LB-MOLE
 THE ENTHALPY OF VAPOR =   39054. BTU/LB-MOLE

PROBLEMS

<u>6-A</u>. In the study of a chemical reaction equilibrium we obtain the following set of simultaneous equations.

$$\left.\begin{array}{l} f_1(x,y) = \dfrac{x(x-y)}{(1-x)(2-x-y)} - 2.667 = 0, \\[4mm] f_2(x,y) = \dfrac{4y^2}{(x-y)(2-x-y)} - 3.20 = 0. \end{array}\right\} \quad (6.A-1)$$

The ranges of the variables are $0 \leqslant x < 1$ and $0 \leqslant y < 1$. There is no physical meaning for values of x or y outside the above ranges. Solve Eq. (6.A-1) by the Newton-Raphson method. (Note: It may be convenient to evaluate the derivatives by a numerical method described in chapter four. In applying the Newton-Raphson method, a bad initial guess may result in $x < 0$, $x \geqslant 1$, $y < 0$, $y \geqslant 1$, or $x = y$. Numerical difficulties may develop if any of the above happens. Therefore steps should be built in your program to terminate the iteration at the first sign of divergence. You may have to run the program more than once, using different initial guesses, to get to the answer.)

Answer: $x = .8342$, $y = .4598$.

<u>6-B</u>. The Wilson equation (1964) is quite accurate for correlation of activity coefficients. For a binary system the activity coefficients are expressed as a function of compositions as follows:

$$\left. \begin{array}{l} \ln \gamma_1 = -\ln(x_1 + Ax_2) + x_2\left(\dfrac{A}{x_1 + Ax_2} - \dfrac{B}{Bx_1 + x_2}\right), \\[4mm] \ln \gamma_2 = -\ln(Bx_1 + x_2) - x_1\left(\dfrac{A}{x_1 + Ax_2} - \dfrac{B}{Bx_1 + x_2}\right), \end{array} \right\} \quad (6.B\text{-}1)$$

where x = mole fraction of a component in the liquid phase,

γ = activity coefficients,

A, B = Wilson parameters.

Subscripts 1 and 2 refer to components 1 and 2, respectively.

In principle, only one experimental point is required to obtain estimates of the parameters.

It is observed that the system menthanol (1)-benzene (2) at one atmosphere (760 mm Hg) pressure exhibits an azeotrope at 58.3°C. At this point the mole fraction of methanol is $x_1 = .61$, and that of benzene is $x_2 = .39$. The vapor pressures of the pure components at 58.3°C are $p_1 = 587.5$ and $p_2 = 368.6$ mm Hg. Neglecting vapor phase imperfection, the activity coefficients at the azeotropic points are

$$\left. \begin{array}{l} \gamma_1 = \dfrac{P}{p_1} = \dfrac{760}{587.5} = 1.2936, \\[4mm] \gamma_2 = \dfrac{P}{p_2} = \dfrac{760}{368.6} = 2.0619. \end{array} \right\} \quad (6.B\text{-}2)$$

The Wilson parameters can be determined from the azeotropic data by substituting the values of activity coefficients and compositions into Eq. (6.B-1) and solving for A and B simultaneously. Solve the problem by the Newton-Raphson method.

(Suggestions: Initial guesses of A = .5 and B = .5 may be
used. Notice that both A and B in Wilson's equation must be
positive. A bad initial guess may result in negative values
of A and B, and the method diverges. Therefore provisions
should be incorporated in your program to terminate the iteration
if either A or B becomes negative.)

Answer: A = .1405, B = .3673.

Chapter 7

Numerical Solution of Ordinary Differential Equations

7.1 Introduction

Because of the complexity of the problems encountered in many chemical engineering processes, the differential equations that arise are often not solvable in terms of elementary functions. In such circumstances, it is necessary to resort to approximate methods. We will consider the Runge-Kutta method, which was one of the earliest methods employed in the numerical solution of differential equations. It is still widely used, and it is easy to program for computer calculations. We will limit our discussion to initial value problems, on the assumption that all information necessary to determine a unique solution of the differential equation is known at the initial point. Numerical solution of boundary value problems are more complex because there are insufficient data to start the integration. They will not be discussed here.

7.2 First Order Differential Equations

Let us consider the first order differential equation of the form

$$\frac{dy}{dx} = f(x,y). \qquad (7.2\text{-}1)$$

The initial condition, $x = x_0$, $y = y_0$, is known.

The well-known fourth-order Runge-Kutta formula is expressed as follows:

$$k_1 = h\, f(x_n, y_n),$$

$$k_2 = h\, f(x_n + h/2, y_n + k_1/2),$$

$$k_3 = h\, f(x_n + h/2, y_n + k_2/2),$$

$$k_4 = h\, f(x_n + h, y_n + k_3),$$

$$x_{n+1} = x_n + h,$$

$$y_{n+1} = y_n + (k_1 + 2k_2 + 2k_3 + k_4)/6.$$

(7.2-2)

The derivation of this set of equations is complex. The reader should consult standard textbooks in mathematics. The calculating procedure involves the choice of a step size h. Then step-by-step integration is performed to determine the increment in y corresponding to the increment in x. In each step the function is evaluated four times for slightly different values of x and y to obtain k_1, k_2, k_3, and k_4, from which the new value of y is calculated. Thus (x_0, y_0) is replaced by (x_1, y_1), and so on. Let us illustrate the use of the Runge-Kutta method in solving a first order differential equation.

EXAMPLE 7.2-1. <u>First Order Differential Equation</u>

Given the differential equation

$$\frac{dy}{dx} = 0.05(1 - e^{.1x}) - 0.05y,$$

with the initial condition y = 0 when x = 0. Find the value of y when x = 60. Solve by the Runge-Kutta method. In order to determine the accuracy of the method, use increments of x, h = 10 and 5. Compare the results.

PROGRAM RUNGE1

Description of Input/Output

The program is formulated according to Eq. (7.2-2). The differential equation must be of the type y' = f(x,y).

XO   -(input) the initial value of x

YO   -(input) the initial value of y

H   -(input) the increment of x, or the step size

NINC   -(input) the number of increments to be carried forward

X   -(output) the value of x after each step

Y   -(output) the corresponding value of y after each step

PROGRAM RUNGE1 (see Table 7-1) was run twice. First, with h = 10 and x = 60 (a given statement of the problem), the value of y was computed to be 0.90283 (see Table 7-2). Second, with h = 5 and x =60, the value of y was computed to be 0.90290. The two values of y are considered to be very close.

7.3 Simultaneous Equations and Equations of Second and Higher Order

The Runge-Kutta method can easily be extended to a system of simultaneous equations of the first order,

$$\left.\begin{array}{l} \dfrac{dy}{dx} = f_1(x,y,z), \\[2mm] \dfrac{dz}{dx} = f_2(x,y,z), \end{array}\right\} \tag{7.3-1}$$

with the initial values x_0, y_0, and z_0 being known.

Table 7-1.   PROGRAM RUNGE1

```
00100      PROGRAM RUNGE1 (INPUT,OUTPUT)
00110C
00120C     THIS PROGRAM SOLVES A FIRST ORDER DIFFERENTIAL EQUATION
00130C     BY THE FOURTH ORDER RUNGE-KUTTA FORMULA.
00140C
00150      REAL K1,K2,K3,K4
00160C
00170C     DEFINE FUNCTION
00180C
00190      F(X,Y)=.05*(1.-EXP(-.1*X))-.05*Y
00200C
00210C     DATA INPUT
00220C
00230      READ*,X0,Y0
00240      READ*,H,NINC
00250      PRINT 1
00260    1 FORMAT(//9X,"X",15X,"Y")
00270      X=X0
00280      Y=Y0
00290      PRINT 5,X,Y
00300    5 FORMAT(2E16.8)
00310C
00320C     RUNGE-KUTTA METHOD
00330C
00350      DO 10 I=1,NINC
00360      K1=H*F(X,Y)
00370      K2=H*F(X+H/2.,Y+K1/2.)
00380      K3=H*F(X+H/2.,Y+K2/2.)
00390      K4=H*F(X+H,Y+K3)
00400      X=X+H
00410      Y=Y+(K1+2.*K2+2.*K3+K4)/6.
00420      PRINT 5,X,Y
00430   10 CONTINUE
00440      STOP
00450      END
```

Table 7-2. An application of PROGRAM RUNGE1

DATA INPUT AT TIME OF EXECUTION

? 0., 0.
? 10., 6

OUTPUT

X	Y
0.	0.
.10000000E+02	.15514269E+00
.20000000E+02	.39977810E+00
.30000000E+02	.60358136E+00
.40000000E+02	.74761110E+00
.50000000E+02	.84249707E+00
.60000000E+02	.90282760E+00

DATA INPUT AT TIME OF EXECUTION

? 0., 0.
? 5., 12

OUTPUT

X	Y
0.	0.
.50000000E+01	.48940795E-01
.10000000E+02	.15483164E+00
.15000000E+02	.27840816E+00
.20000000E+02	.39958377E+00
.25000000E+02	.50907909E+00
.30000000E+02	.60352739E+00
.35000000E+02	.68264787E+00
.40000000E+02	.74764192E+00
.45000000E+02	.80030648E+00
.50000000E+02	.84256344E+00
.55000000E+02	.87622643E+00
.60000000E+02	.90290013E+00

The Runge-Kutta formulas become

$$k_1 = h\, f_1(x_n, y_n, z_n),$$

$$l_1 = h\, f_2(x_n, y_n, z_n),$$

$$k_2 = h\, f_1\left(x_n + \frac{h}{2}, y_n + \frac{k_1}{2}, z_n + \frac{l_1}{2}\right),$$

$$l_2 = h\, f_2\left(x_n + \frac{h}{2}, y_n + \frac{k_1}{2}, z_n + \frac{l_1}{2}\right),$$

$$k_3 = h\, f_1\left(x_n + \frac{h}{2}, y_n + \frac{k_2}{2}, z_n + \frac{l_2}{2}\right),$$

$$l_3 = h\, f_2\left(x_n + \frac{h}{2}, y_n + \frac{k_2}{2}, z_n + \frac{l_2}{2}\right), \qquad (7.3\text{-}2)$$

$$k_4 = h\, f_1(x_n + h, y_n + k_3, z_n + l_3),$$

$$l_4 = h\, f_2(x_n + h, y_n + k_3, z_n + l_3),$$

$$x_{n+1} = x_n + h,$$

$$y_{n+1} = y_n + (k_1 + 2k_2 + 2k_3 + k_4)/6,$$

$$z_{n+1} = z_n + (l_1 + 2l_2 + 2l_3 + l_4)/6.$$

Eq. (7.3-2) can be employed to solve equations of second and higher order, since a single differential equation of higher order can always be replaced by an equivalent system of first order equations. In considering an equation of second order,

$$\frac{d^2 y}{dx^2} = f\left(x, y, \frac{dy}{dx}\right), \qquad (7.3\text{-}3)$$

let

$$\frac{dy}{dx} = z. \qquad (7.3\text{-}4)$$

Eq. (7.3-3) becomes

$$\frac{dz}{dx} = f(x,y,z).$$

(7.3-5)

Eqs. (7.3-4) and (7.3-5) are a system of first order equations equivalent to the second order equation represented by Eq. (7.3-3). Substituting the given functions into Eq. (7.3-2), we have

$$k_1 = h\, z_n,$$

$$l_1 = h\, f(x_n, y_n, z_n),$$

$$k_2 = h\, (z_n + \frac{l_1}{2}),$$

$$l_2 = h\, f(x_n + \frac{h}{2}, y_n + \frac{k_1}{2}, z_n + \frac{l_1}{2}),$$

$$k_3 = h\, (z_n + \frac{l_2}{2}),$$

$$l_3 = h\, f(x_n + \frac{h}{2}, y_n + \frac{k_2}{2}, z_n + \frac{l_2}{2}),$$

(7.3-6)

$$k_4 = h\, (z_n + l_3),$$

$$l_4 = h\, f(x_n + h, y_n + k_3, z_n + l_3),$$

$$x_{n+1} = x_n + h,$$

$$y_{n+1} = y_n + (k_1 + 2k_2 + 2k_3 + k_4)/6,$$

$$z_{n+1} = z_n + (l_1 + 2l_2 + 2l_3 + l_4)/6.$$

In Eq. (7.3-6), if we substitute the expressions for the k's into the expressions for the l's, the following set of recurrence formulas results:

$$l_1 = h \ f(x_n, y_n, z_n),$$

$$l_2 = h \ f(x_n + \frac{h}{2}, y_n + \frac{hz_n}{2}, \ z_n + \frac{l_1}{2}),$$

$$l_3 = h \ f(x_n + \frac{h}{2}, y_n + \frac{hz_n}{2} + \frac{hl_1}{4}, z_n + \frac{l_2}{2}),$$

$$l_4 = h \ f(x_n + h, y_n + hz_n + \frac{hl_2}{2}, z_n + l_3),$$

$$x_{n+1} = x_n + h,$$

$$y_{n+1} = y_n + hz_n + h(l_1 + l_2 + l_3)/6,$$

$$z_{n+1} = z_n + (l_1 + 2l_2 + 2l_3 + l_4)/6.$$

$$(7.3-7)$$

EXAMPLE 7.3-1. Second Order Differential Equation

Given the differential equation

$$y'' = 2y' - y + 3xe^{-x}$$

with initial conditions $y_0 = 0$, $y_0' = 1$, when $x_0 = 0$. Find the value of y when x = 1. Solve the equation twice, with h = 0.1 and 0.2. Compare the results.

PROGRAM RUNGE2

Description of Input/Output

XO   -(input) the initial value of x

YO   -(input) the initial value of y

ZO   -(input) the initial value of the derivative, dy/dx

H   -(input) the increment of x

NINC   -(input) the number of increments

Table 7-3. PROGRAM RUNGE2

```
00100       PROGRAM RUNGE2 (INPUT,OUTPUT)
00110C
00120C      THIS PROGRAM SOLVES A SECOND ORDER DIFFERENTIAL EQUATION
00130C      BY THE FOURTH ORDER RUNGE-KUTTTA FORMULA.
00140C
00150       REAL L1,L2,L3,L4
00160C
00170C      DEFINE FUNCTION
00180C
00190       F(X,Y,Z)=2.*Z-Y+3.*X*EXP(-X)
00200C
00210C      DATA INPUT
00220C
00230       READ*,X0,Y0,Z0
00240       READ*,H,NINC
00250       PRINT 1
00260     1 FORMAT(//10X,"X",15X,"Y",15X,"Z")
00270       X=X0
00280       Y=Y0
00290       Z=Z0
00300       PRINT 5,X,Y,Z
00310     5 FORMAT(3E16.8)
00320C
00330C      RUNGE-KUTTA METHOD
00340C
00350       DO 10 I=1,NINC
00360       L1=H*F(X,Y,Z)
00370       L2=H*F(X+H/2.,Y+H*Z/2.,Z+L1/2.)
00380       L3=H*F(X+H/2.,Y+H*Z/2.+H*L1/4.,Z+L2/2.)
00390       L4=H*F(X+H,Y+H*Z+H*L2/2.,Z+L3)
00400       X=X+H
00410       Y=Y+H*Z+H*(L1+L2+L3)/6.
00420       Z=Z+(L1+2.*L2+2.*L3+L4)/6.
00430       PRINT 5,X,Y,Z
00440    10 CONTINUE
00450       STOP
00460       END
```

Table 7-4. An application of PROGRAM RUNGE2

DATA INPUT AT TIME OF EXECUTION

? 0., 0., 1.
? .2, 5

OUTPUT

X	Y	Z
0.	0.	.10000000E+01
.20000000E+00	.24824795E+00	.15260164E+01
.40000000E+00	.62913324E+00	.23348547E+01
.60000000E+00	.12050139E+01	.34881192E+01
.80000000E+00	.20528857E+01	.50712993E+01
.10000000E+01	.32696354E+01	.71987735E+01

DATA INPUT AT TIME OF EXECUTION

? 0., 0., 1.
? .1, 10

OUTPUT

X	Y	Z
0.	0.	.10000000E+01
.10000000E+00	.11101606E+00	.12307109E+01
.20000000E+00	.24829332E+00	.15260796E+01
.30000000E+00	.41857432E+00	.18918435E+01
.40000000E+00	.62923734E+00	.23349959E+01
.50000000E+00	.88842706E+00	.28638900E+01
.60000000E+00	.12051965E+01	.34883610E+01
.70000000E+00	.15896621E+01	.42198708E+01
.80000000E+00	.20531749E+01	.50716740E+01
.90000000E+00	.26085087E+01	.60590108E+01
.10000000E+01	.32700697E+01	.71993259E+01

X   -(output) the value of x after each step of integration

Y   -(output) the value of y after each step of integration
        (The last value of y is the desired result.)

Z   -(output) the value of dy/dx after each step of
        integration

PROGRAM RUNGE2 (see Table 7-3) was written to solve the given second order differential equation by Eq. (7.3-7). Two successive runs were made. The results are given in Table 7-4.

With h = 0.2 and x = 1, the value of y was computed to be 3.2696. With h = 0.1 and x =1, the value of y was computed to be 3.2701. The two values of y are considered to be very close.

It must be pointed out that the examples cited herein are not at all typical. The solutions obtained by the numerical method are approximate, not exact. Sometimes the result is very bad. The possibility of errors in numerical methods is what the user should be constantly aware of.

7.4 Gear's Method

The two best-known classes of methods for the numerical solution of initial value problems are the Runge-Kutta and the predictor-corrector methods. Gear's method is the most modern predictor-corrector method. It has built-in procedures for starting the solution, estimating the errors, adjusting the step size, and selecting the order as the computation proceeds.

Thus the amount of computational work is minimized for a given error tolerance. The method uses the Adams-Bashford-Moulton predictor-corrector pairs (Methods of orders one to eight are available.) and incorporates a sophisticated iterative solution of the corrector equation. The algorithm also includes a special approach suitable for the solution of a stiff system of differential equations.

Since there are many open questions concerning error, stability, and convergence, the criteria for deciding on the best order and step size are very complicated. Some detailed treatments are found in Gear (1971(b)) and Lambert (1973).

Gear's method requires a great amount of programming. Since a complete description of the algorithm has been made available (Gear, 1971(a) and (b)), we recommend that the packaged subroutines be used, if possible.

7.5 Comparison of Methods

The Runge-Kutta method is self-starting, simple, easy to program and yields reasonably accurate results. The estimation of error in Runge-Kutta formulas may be complicated because of nonlinearity. However, in practice this seldom poses a problem. The classical Runge-Kutta method with a fixed step size is one of the most convenient methods for the solution of engineering problems on a computer. We can always run the program with two different step sizes. If the answers stay reasonably close, they can usually be considered accurate.

In this elementary book, efficient programming is not our concern. We do not intend to develop highly efficient and fool-proof programs to be used at computer centers. Our main goal is to get familiar with the method and its applications so as to amplify our own arsenal of numerical computation. As a matter of fact, most of our problems will use little computer time, even with an inefficient method of solution. It may not be worthwhile to invest a large amount of human effort in programming, only to save a fraction of a second of computer time.

For large problems in which good accuracy is required, the increased speed of multi-step methods over Runge-Kutta methods is significant. Besides, the Runge-Kutta methods are inadequate for dealing with stiff equations. By contrast, Gear's method becomes the most effective numerical technique. Especially if the computer library contains canned subroutines, then such programs should be used to our advantage.

PROBLEM

7-A. Consider a simple reaction mechanism of the following type
in which a first-order reaction is followed by a second-order
reaction

$$A \xrightarrow{k_1} B, \qquad\qquad (7.A-1)$$

$$A + B \xrightarrow{k_2} C. \qquad\qquad (7.A-2)$$

The differential reaction rate equations are

$$-\frac{d[A]}{dt} = k_1[A] + k_2[A][B] , \qquad\qquad (7.A-3)$$

$$\frac{d[B]}{dt} = k_1[A] - k_2[A][B] , \qquad\qquad (7.A-4)$$

$$\frac{d[C]}{dt} = k_2[A][B] = -\frac{1}{2}\left(\frac{d[A]}{dt} + \frac{d[B]}{dt}\right), \qquad (7.A-5)$$

where   A, B, C = components A, B, and C, respectively,

k_1, k_2 = specific reaction rate constants,

t = time.

The square brackets denote concentration. The positive sign
means increase in amount and the negative sign means decrease.

Given that k_1 = 0.1, k_2 = 0.05 and the initial values at
time t = 0: $[A]_0$ = 1, $[B]_0$ = $[C]_0$ = 0. Find values of [A], [B],
and [C] at time t = 60.

(Note: The above set of equations is nonlinear and cannot be
readily integrated. Solve Eqs. (7.A-3) and (7.A-4) for [A] and

[B] by the Runge-Kutta method. The variable [C] is dependent.
Once the values of [A] and [B] are established, [C] can be
obtained from

$$[C] = \frac{[A]_0 - [A] - [B]}{2} . \qquad (7.A-6)$$

Eq. (7.A-6) can be derived by multiplying (7.A-5) by dt and
integrating between the initial and final values.)

Answers: At t = 60, [A] =.0004, [B] = .6886, [C] = .1555
(with step size, the increment of t, h = 2).

Chapter 8

Plotting

8.1 Plot of a Single-Valued Function $y = f(x)$

Graphical representation often provides a good overall picture of the nature of data. Thus it is desirable to produce a point plot of the results of a calculation or of a set of experimental data. The following example illustrates how such a plot can be produced on the line printer or the typewriter.

EXAMPLE 8.1-1. Plot of an X-Y Diagram

Given the following relations of x and y

x	y
.02	.04
.58	.78
.26	.46
.13	.26
.43	.63

Plot the data in the x-y plane.

The following general procedure is useful.

(a) We choose the variable y to decrease down the page in the vertical direction and the variable x to increase across the page from left to right. (Sometimes it is more convenient to choose y as the transverse axis and x as the vertical axis.)

(b) By examining the data, we can see that the range of x is between 0 and .6 and the range of y is between 0 and .8.

(c) Suppose the plot is to consist of 40 lines with 60 characters per line. We scale the data so that all points will be inside the diagram. The scaling of the ordinates is done as follows:

$$IX(J)=X(J)*100.+.5,$$
$$IY(J)=Y(J)*50.+.5,$$

where IX = column index of the data point,

IY = line index of the data point.

Since the range of X is 0--.6, (.6 - 0) x 100 = 60. Sixty characters will cover the whole width of X. Since the range of Y is 0--.8, (.8 - 0) x 50 = 40. Forty lines will contain all the Y's. The addition of .5 rounds off the value to the nearest whole number. This is necessary so that each character will occupy one space and each line number will be an integer.

(d) We use two print symbols, an asterisk "*" and a blank " ". The plot starts at the top. The line index is initially set at 40 and is decreased to zero by steps of one. When a line is printed, it will usually contain blank characters only. However, on a particular line where the data point is to appear (as indicated by the line index IY), an asterisk (*) is printed in the position indicated by the column index IX. The y-axis and the annotations are

215

printed along with the data point according to appropriate FORMAT statements. After all forty lines are printed, the x-axis and its annotations are printed according to appropriate FORMAT statements.

The above method is straightforward. A flow diagram of the plotting procedure is given in Figure 8-1. PROGRAM PLOT1 follows the flow diagram.

PROGRAM PLOT1

Description of Input/Output

ISTAR - print symbol "*", entered under the DATA statement

IBLANK- print symbol " ", entered under the DATA statement

N   -(input) the number of data points

X   -(input) one-dimensional array containing values of
           the independent variable

Y   -(input) one-dimensional array containing the corre-
           sponding values of the dependent variable

IX   -(intermediate calculation) one-dimensional array
           containing the column indexes of the data points

IY   -(intermediate calculation) one-dimensional array
           containing the corresponding line indexes of the
           data points

LINE -(output) one-dimensional array containing the characters
           of a line

XA   -(output) one-dimensional array containing the annota-
           tions of the x-axis

YA   -(output) the annotation of the y-axis

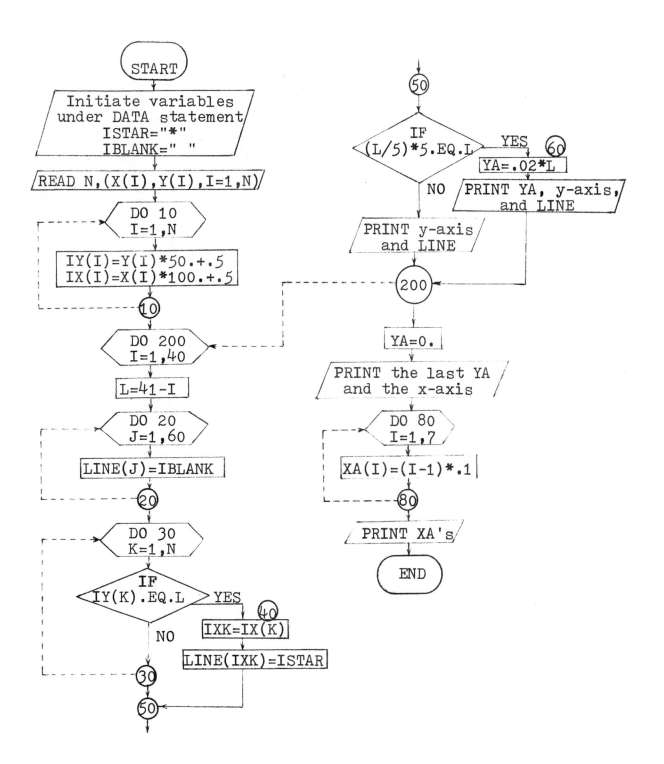

Figure 8-1. Flow diagram of PLOT1

PROGRAM PLOT1 (see Table 8-1) was run. The computer

printout (see Table 8-2) was taken from a typewriter, the

LA36 DEC Writer II, at the time-sharing terminal of the

University of Lowell. It must be pointed out that a plot

like this can be produced much more efficiently on a line

printer, which has more print positions per line and much

higher speed.

Often we need to plot two or more functions on the same

diagram so as to compare their values. It is not much more

difficult to do so, once the problem of scaling is solved.

Naturally, a different print symbol will be used to represent

each function, and provisions will be made so that, at

locations where two or more functions have the same value,

only one point will be printed.

Table 8-1. PROGRAM PLOT1

```
00100        PROGRAM PLOT1 (INPUT,OUTPUT)
00110        DIMENSION LINE(60),X(10),Y(10),IX(10),IY(10),XA(7)
00120        DATA ISTAR,IBLANK/"*"," "/
00130C
00140C      INPUT
00150C
00160        READ*,N,(X(I),Y(I),I=1,N)
00170C
00180C      SCALING - COMPUTING THE LINE INDEX AND COLUMN INDEX
00190C      OF EACH DATA POINT TO BE PRINTED
00200C
00210        DO 10 I=1,N
00220        IY(I)=Y(I)*50.+.5
00230     10 IX(I)=X(I)*100.+.5
00240C
00250C      START PRINTING AT THE TOP.   EACH TIME L IS DECREMENTED
00260C      BY ONE.
00270C
00280        PRINT 1
00290      1 FORMAT(///)
00300        DO 200 I=1,40
00310        L=41-I
00320C
00330C      INITIATE LINE WITH ALL BLANK CHARACTERS.
00340C
00350        DO 20 J=1,60
00360     20 LINE(J)=IBLANK
00370C
00380C      MATCH LINE NO. WITH LINE INDEX OF A POINT TO FIND
00390C      WHERE A STAR IS TO BE PRINTED.
00400C
00410        DO 30 K=1,N
00420        IF(IY(K).EQ.L) GO TO 40
00430     30 CONTINUE
00440        GO TO 50
00450     40 IXK=IX(K)
00460        LINE(IXK)=ISTAR
00470C
00480C      EVERY FIFTH LINE BEARS THE ANNOTATION OF THE Y-AXIS.
00490C
00500     50 IF((L/5)*5.EQ.L) GO TO 60
00510        PRINT 100,LINE
00520    100 FORMAT(7X,".",60A1)
00530        GO TO 200
00540C
00550C      GENERATE THE ANNOTATION OF THE Y-AXIS.
00560C
00570     60 YA=.02*L
00580        PRINT 101,YA,LINE
00590    101 FORMAT(1X,F4.2,2X,"+",60A1)
00600    200 CONTINUE
00610C
00620C      PRINT THE X-AXIS.
00630C
00640        YA=0.
00650        PRINT 102,YA
00660    102 FORMAT(1X,F4.2,2X,6("+........."),"+")
```

```
00668C
00670C        GENERATE THE ANNOTATIONS OF THE X-AXIS.
00680C        EVERY TENTH SPACE BEARS AN ANNOTATION.
00690C
00700         DO 80 I=1,7
00710      80 XA(I)=(I-1)*.1
00720         PRINT 103,XA
00730     103 FORMAT(/,7F10.2)
00740         STOP
00750         END
```

Table 8-2. An application of PROGRAM PLOT1

DATA INPUT AT TIME OF EXECUTION
? 5
? .02,.04, .58,.78, .26,.46, .13,.26, .41,.63
OUTPUT

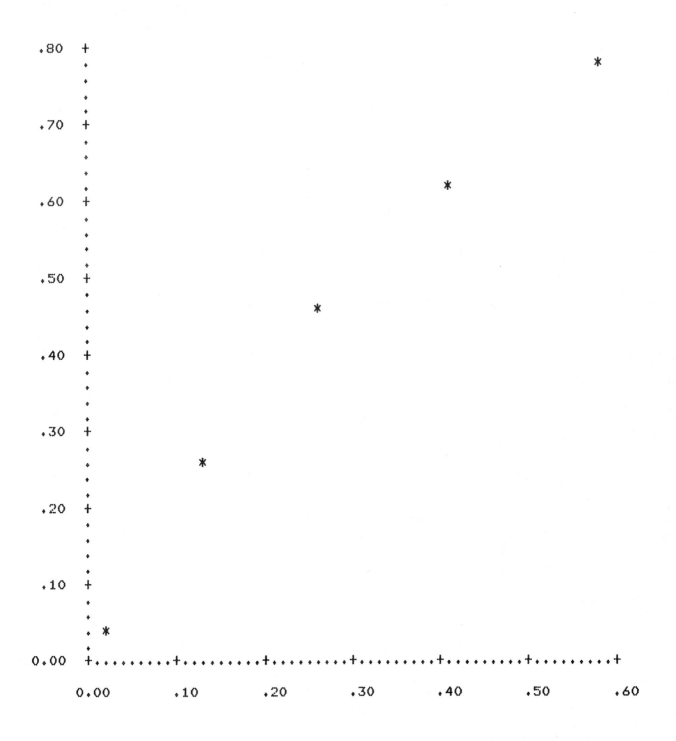

PROBLEM

8-A. Solution of Prob. 7-A by the Runge-Kutta method has
generated the following information:

Time	[A]	[B]	[C]
0	1.0	0	0
1	.9027	.0929	.0022
2	.8113	.1728	.0079
5	.5773	.3523	.0352
10	.3131	.5215	.0827
20	.0854	.6461	.1342
30	.0225	.6777	.1499
40	.0059	.6859	.1541
50	.0015	.6880	.1552
60	.0004	.6886	.1555

Write a computer program to plot [A], [B], and [C] vs. time.

Postface

Coming to the end of the text, the reader has seen numerous examples that illustrate the application of numerical methods to computer solution of typical chemical engineering problems. In this introductory book, we have confined ourselves to very simple cases. It is hoped that enough interest has been aroused so that the reader will want to explore more challenging problems using more sophisticated methods.

There is a large number of programs for advanced problems to be found in various books and technical journals. The most comprehensive compilation of computer programs for chemical engineers comes in the seven volumes of Computer Programs for Chemical Engineering Education, edited by the CACHE Committee and published by Sterling Swift Publishing Company, Manchaca, Texas (1972). Chemical Engineering, a McGraw-Hill publication, has kept an up-to-date list of computer programs of interest to chemical engineers. The listing contains such basic information as program name, description, author, address, etc., but not the program itself. Reprints of the listing are available from Chemical Engineering.

A number of library subroutines are available, such as NAG (Numerical Algorithms Group - originated in Great Britian), SSP (Scientific Subroutine Package - IBM), SPSS (a statistical package), EISPACK (a collection of subroutines for matrix

eigenvalue problems), and NRCC (National Resource for Computation
in Chemistry - Lawrence Berkeley Laboratory). One would need
background information to gain access to these sources and to
use them.

APPENDIX

Classification of Errors

Numerical methods are methods of approximations. There
are three sources of errors.

(1) Roundoff error

Since computer calculations are limited to a certain
number of digits, the remaining digits will be chopped off.
This introduces roundoff error. Roundoff errors are particularly
enhanced when two nearly equal numbers are subtracted. Some
computers allow the use of double-precision arithmetic to
reduce the incidents of roundoff errors. However, such usage
should be avoided unless it is necessary, because double-
precision arithmetic uses additional memory spaces and reduces
computation speed. A preferred approach is to modify a part of
the program so as to lessen the effect of roundoff errors.
The partial pivoting technique mentioned in Sec. 2.2 is a good
example.

(2) Truncation error

Very often we have to use an approximation formula.
Consider the Taylor's series,

$$f(x) = f(x_0) + f'(x_0)(x-x_0) + \frac{f''(x_0)}{2!} (x-x_0)^2 + \ldots$$

It is impossible to sum an infinite number of terms. If we
choose to approximate the function by using only the first

two terms and discarding the rest, a truncation error results. Newton's method of Sec. 1.3 is an example. We can see that the error is of the order of $(x - x_0)^2$ if $(x - x_0)$ is small.

(3) Inherited error

Certain calculations may depend on the results of previous calculations. Error is produced by errors occurring in previous steps. The way in which errors accumulate and propagate depends on the type of mathematical operation and the functional relationship.

Error analysis is valuable in that it provides a means to estimate the accuracy of the answer and gives insight to compare numerical methods or to devise an improved method. We encourage our readers to pursue the matter by reading some standard textbooks on numerical analysis.

A satisfactory method of dealing with error is complicated. It becomes even more difficult when the accuracy is dependent on the particular numerical method and on the particular problem to be solved. Since this book covers only relatively simple programs at an elementary level, our primary concern is clear and logical presentation. Mathematical rigor and elegance is not an object of idolatry. Instead of spending much time in lengthy discussions of rigorous error analysis, we choose the application-oriented approach. We believe that the best way to learn computer programming is actually to run the program.

With the advent of the time-sharing systems the user can interact directly with the computer. It is relatively easy to make modifications or corrections during a run. In most of our sample programs we purposely command the computer to print out the intermediate calculations. In this way the computer is called upon to help with error analysis. We are able to extract useful information as to the accuracy of the answer by observing how the calculation converges. Computer programmed examples are also given to solve the same problem using different methods (e.g., Examples 1.2-1 and 1.3-1). They offer a comparison of methods as to their relative effectiveness. Nearly identical answers convince us of the validity of the solution. In Examples 4.2-1 and 4.3-1 we have verified the accuracy by varying the step size. Further, these two examples show that the truncation error in integration by Simpson's rule is less than that by the trapezoid rule. Both methods are generally good.

Another kind of error, which is not related to any of the above, may be called the error of method. In the curve-fitting problem of Examples 3.1-2 and 3.3-2, we can see that the choice of the type of equation is of primary importance. A chemical engineer must have sufficient and clear understanding of the principles involved before he can successfully apply mathematics as a tool to obtain a meaningful and usable solution.

REFERENCES

1. Amundson, N. R. (1966): "Mathematical Methods in Chemical Engineering," Prentice-Hall, Englewood Cliffs, N. J.

2. CACHE (1972): "Computer Programs for Chemical Engineering Education," 7 vols., edited by CACHE, Sterling Swift Pub. Co., Manchaca, Texas.

3. Calingaert, G. and Davis, D. S. (1925): Ind. Eng. Chem., vol. 17, p. 1287.

4. Carnahan, B., Luther, H. A., and Wilkes, J. O. (1969): "Applied Numerical Methods," Wiley, New York.

5. Carslaw, H. S. and Jaeger, J. C. (1959): "Conduction of Heat in Solids," 2nd. ed., Oxford University Press, London.

6. Conte, S. D. and de Boor, C. (1980): "Elementary Numerical Analysis: An Algorithmic Approach," 3rd. ed., McGraw-Hill, New York.

7. Crank, J. (1956): "The Mathematics of Diffusion," Oxford University Press, London.

8. DePriester, C. L. (1953): Chem. Eng. Prog. Symposium Series, no. 7, pp. 1-43, AIChE, New York.

9. Dorn, W. S. and McCracken, D. D. (1972): "Numerical Methods with Fortran IV Case Studies," Wiley, New York.

10. Forsythe, G. E., Malcolm, M. A., and Moler, C. B. (1977): "Computer Methods for Mathematical Computations," Prentice-Hall, Englewood Cliffs, N. J.

11. Forsythe, G. E. and Moler, C. B. (1967): "Computer Solution of Linear Algebraic Systems," Prentice-Hall, Englewood Cliffs, N. J.

12. Francis, J. G. F. (1961/62): "The QR Transformation," Comp. J., vol. 4, pp. 265-271, pp. 332-345.

13. Gear, C. W. (1971a): "The Automatic Integration of Ordinary Differential Equations," Communications of the Association for Computing Machinery, vol. 14, pp. 176-190.

14. Gear, C. W. (1971b): "Numerical Initial Value Problems in Ordinary Differential Equations," Prentice-Hall, Englewood Cliffs, N. J.

15. Gerald, C. F. (1970): "Applied Numerical Analysis," Addison-Wesley, Reading, Mass.

16. Hamming, R. W. (1973): "Numerical Methods for Scientists and Engineers," 2nd. ed., McGraw-Hill, New York.

17. Hildebrand, F. B. (1974): "Introduction to Numerical Analysis," 2nd. ed., McGraw-Hill, New York.

18. Holland, C. D. (1975): "Fundamentals and Modeling of Separation Processes," Prentice-Hall, Englewood Cliffs, N. J.

19. Hornbeck, R. W. (1975): "Numerical Methods," Quantum Pub. Inc., New York.

20. Householder, A. S. (1953): "Principles of Numerical Analysis," McGraw-Hill, New York.

21. Issacson, E. and Keller, H. B. (1966): "Analysis of Numerical Methods," Wiley, New York.

22. King, C. J. (1980): "Separation Processes," 2nd. ed., McGraw-Hill, New York.

23. Lambert, J. D. (1973): "Computational Methods in Ordinary Differential Equations," Wiley, New York.

24. McCracken, D. D. and Dorn, W. S. (1964): "Numerical Methods and Fortran Programming," Wiley, New York.

25. Molokanov, Y. K., Korabline, T. P., Mazurina, N. I., and Nikiforov, G. A. (1972): International Chem. Eng., vol. 12, no. 2, p. 209.

26. Moody, L. F. (1944): Trans. ASME, vol. 66, p. 133.

27. Muller, D. E. (1956): Math. Table Aids Comp., vol. 10, p. 208.

28. Ostrowski, A. M. (1966): "Solution of Equations and Systems of Equations," Academic Press, New York.

29. Pham, Q. T. (1979): Trans. IChE, vol. 57, p. 281.

30. Rachford, H. H., Jr. and Rice, J. D. (1952): J. Petrol. Tech., vol. 4, no. 10, p. 19.

31. Ralston, A. and Rabinowitz, P. (1978): "A First Course in Numerical Analysis," 2nd. ed., McGraw-Hill, New York.

32. Ralston, A. and Wilf, H. S. (1960): "Mathematical Methods for Digital Computers," vol. 1, Wiley, New York.

33. Ralston, A. and Wilf, H. S. (1967): "Mathematical Methods for Digital Computers," vol. 2, Wiley, New York.

34. Redlich, O. and Kwong, J. N. S. (1949): Chem. Rev., vol. 44, p. 233.

35. Rutishauser, R. (1958): "Solution of Eigenvalue Problems with the LR Transformation," National Bureau of Standards, Applied Mathematics Series, no. 49, pp. 47-81.

36. Scarborough, J. B. (1966): "Numerical Mathematical Analysis," 6th. ed., Johns Hopkins Press, Baltimore.

37. Schwarz, H. R., Rutishauser, H., and Stiefel, E. (Translated by Hertelendy, F., 1973): "Numerical Analysis of Symmetric Matrices," Prentice-Hall, Englewood Cliffs, N. J.

38. Traub, J. F. (1964): "Iterative Methods for the Solution of Equations," Prentice-Hall, Englewood Cliffs, N. J.

39. Underwood, A. J. V. (1948): Chem. Eng. Prog., vol. 44, p. 603.

40. Wang, J. C. and Henke, G. E. (1966): "Tridiagonal Matrix for Distillation," Hydrocarbon Processing, vol. 45, no. 8, p. 155.

41. Weast, R. C. (editor, 1968): "Handbook of Chemistry and Physics," 49th. ed., The Chemical Rubber Pub. Co., Cleveland, Ohio.

42. Wilkinson, J. H. (1964): "Rounding Errors in Algebraic Processes," Prentice-Hall, Englewood Cliffs, N. J.

43. Wilkinson, J. H. (1965): "The Algebraic Eigenvalue Problem," Oxford University Press, London.

44. Williams, P. W. (1973): "Numerical Computation," Barnes and Noble, New York.

45. Wilson, G. M. (1964): J. Am. Chem. Soc., vol. 86, p. 127.

INDEX

Time-sharing systems, iv, 11, 218

Trapezoid rule, 147

Tridiagonal matrix, 84

Two-dimensional array, storing of data in, 168

Turbulent flow, explicit equation for, 60

Underwood equation, 3

Vapor-liquid equilibrium ratio constant, correlation of, 143

Vapor pressure correlation, 105, 136

Virial equation of state, 7, 13

Wilson equation, 196